Holt High Street, 1909

Foreword

The history of Holt is fascinating because the town has, over the years, mirrored national economic and social trends and attitudes.

In my original research I was fortunate to receive the help of many local people and their names are recorded in the Foreword to the first edition. For this new edition I have received unstinting help from Mrs Janice Greaves, Clerk to the Town Council; Mr Michael Hill, Mr Philip High and Mr Norman Cockaday of the Town Council; Mr David Brieger of the Holt Chamber of Trade; Mr Michael Barrett of Gresham's School; Mr Stephen Benson of the Holt Society; Mrs Joyce Belding of the Holt History Group; and Mr Gary Alexander of the Planning Department, North Norfolk District Council. My special thanks are also due to Mrs Elsie Checkley for permission to use photographs from her late husband's collection. Any omissions or errors are mine.

In a text of this length it is impossible to do more than scratch the surface of the town's history and development; I hope, howwever, that what is recorded will be of interest and Michael Barrett's forthcoming book,which will take a more detailed look at the history of this attractive town, is awaited with great interest. In the meantime I will always be pleased to hear from anyone who can add anything to what is recorded or suggest new avenues to be explored.

5 Abbey Road, Sheringham NR26 8HH   **Peter Brooks**

Early history

Apart from the Great Fire of 1708, which destroyed much of the town centre, Holt has changed relatively little over the centuries. Indeed, anyone returning from the early 18th century would be immediately at home. True, the shop fronts have changed, the roads and pavements are eminently more passable, street lighting is more efficient and the traffic more frightening, but the heart of the town will still be clearly recognizable.

The name 'Holt' is thought to derive from the Saxon word for wood. It was at a meeting place of tracks and roads that the first settlement began in a wooded clearing on this high ground of North Norfolk, an environment still in existence in 1205 when Simon FitzSiman was paying 2 hawks a year to King John for the right to hunt in Holt and Cley woods.

The town is first mentioned in the Domesday Book (1086) when it was credited with five water-mills, a market and, interestingly, its own port of Cley which was attached to the Holt Manor. This situation existed certainly to 1790 when the *Universal British Directory* recorded that 'all the grocery etc. sent to this town by sea, is shipped from Harrison's wharfe, St Catherine's to Blakeney or Cley, the nearest sea ports'. It was peopled by 10 freemen, 48 smallholders and two serfs who between them could call on 12 plough-teams and the produce of 20 hogs and 90 sheep; there was also one solitary carthorse. It was held of the King by Walter Giffard and then passed to Hugh, Earl of Chester who let it to the De Vaux family. The Manor paid just £66 per annum in rent, with part of it taking the form of a day's groceries for the Lord's household or, as the chronicler of the time picturesquely put it, 'honey for one night'.

The earliest known written records of a church dedicated to St Andrew date from 1288, and the 1988 Holt Festival celebrated this service to the town. We know the church was rebuilt in the 14th century by Sir William de Nerford and his wife, Petronilla, and some of the materials used then survive today in the tower and chancel.

There is, unfortunately, little recorded history of the town's development during medieval times although Lewis Radford, in his *History of Holt* (1908) gives us many an interesting glimpse into the activities of local individuals.

Without its market, and the two fairs on 25th April and 25th November, Holt would probably have slipped into relative obscurity for it was these that brought custom and life into the town and led to the settlement we see today. Indeed, in many old documents, the town is referred to as 'Holt-Markett'. Prior to the fire of 1708 the market stretched over some two acres and was originally a separate property. Radford recalls, for example, that in 1190 it was held by Hamon of Hempstead and later by Hugh de Cayley who held it of the Crown at a rent of 20 shillings. Early documents relating to the sale of the premises recently

Fish Hill: an old shop in Holt Market, recently known as The Coffee Pot

known as The Coffee Pot refer to it as being in the Manor of Holt Market. It has been a cordwainer's shop and occupied by a basket maker and butcher and originally comprised '2 messuages, formerly one, with shop, warehouse, cellars, stables, other edifices, yard and appurtenances'.

The market-place was also the place where, during the period of the Commonwealth (1654–1658), marriage banns were proclaimed and where, no doubt, local 'tokens' were used as currency. These were small copper coins issued by tradesmen and in Norfolk some 325 varieties, bearing 57 place names, are known. In Holt one bore the name 'Francis Shawe in Hallt 1658' and carried the impression of a man making candles, while the other was marked 'Daniel Roll of Holt 1666' and bore the imprint of a mortar.

In those medieval days lawlessness and disorder were only too rife, truly a time of survival of the fittest – or the more influential. At Holt bailiffs of the Lord of the Manor, Sir John de Vaux, were guilty of many misdeeds, including stealing food and clothing from stall-holders, robbing visitors to the market and enticing horses, cattle and fowls onto land belonging to their master – and then demanding exorbitant sums for their release.

But it was not just at local level that misdemeanors were common. Alice Perers, daughter of John and Gunnora Perers of the Perers Manor in the town, although married to Sir John Nerford, became the mistress of Edward III while in the service of his wife, Queen Philippa. When the Queen died Edward gave her jewels and many valuables and for several years she led the dissipations at the Royal Court, it not being until 1376 that the Black Prince finally succeeded in banning her. She returned in 1377 during the King's illness and is credited with stealing the rings from his fingers as he lay on his deathbed; she then married her former lover, Sir William Windsor, whose influence was instrumental in having some of her former properties returned.

The plague of 1348 swept through the county, taking with it 23 priests in the Holt deanery. The Peasants' Revolt, some 33 years later, was to involve Holt, for followers of the local leader Geoffrey Litster of Felmingham preached sedition in the Market Place and were ably backed by 'that unscrupulous and unquiet knight, Sir Roger Bacon of Baconsthorpe'. Radford refers to Litster capturing Sir Stephen Hales, Lord of the Manor of Holt Hales, and compelling him to work as a menial. This outrage is attributed to the work of Sir Roger, and was accompanied by local acts of pillage, common robbery and the burning of the manor rolls to destroy proofs of titles to property and of tenants' obligations. The revolt was put down by Henry Despenser, Bishop of Norwich, who swept through Eastern England capturing, condemning, absolving and hanging the ringleaders, including Litster. This crusading prelate was known as 'Fighting Henry' and was remembered in the name of a public house in the Market Place (now known more prosaically as The Railway Tavern).

Poverty

The Holt church registers begin in March 1558 and provide much information on everyday life in the town. Interestingly many of the early names survive today – Baker, Chapman, Crowe, Fuller, King and Preston, for example. In 1588, the year of the Spanish Armada, it is recorded that nearby Weybourne was being fortified with a 'continnuall garrison of men bothe of horse and foote with skonces [earthworks], ordinaunce and all manner of warlyke appoyntments to defende the Spannyardes landinge theare'. It is not difficult to imagine the excitement and activity that must have spread throughout the town.

With widespread poverty to contend with, Elizabeth's Parliament passed the country's first Poor Law and in Holt the register records, in 1599, that 'In this yeare was the house for the poore builded by the Towne'. It was built on what *Holt heath* was then the heath and there is some argument as to whether this was near the *in 1819* site of the old gas works at the top of Letheringsett Hill or on the site of the new

House of Industry, built in 1799. The latter building was sold in 1839 for £1,239, the proceeds (less £545 to pay off the outstanding mortgage) being applied to the local Poor Rate. It survives today as a collection of six cottages on the corner of Pearsons Road and Grove Lane, although the 50 or so acres awarded by the Inclosure Act have long since gone for other purposes. In Holt, as elsewhere, the occupants were expected to work for their shelter and keep, so the official title of 'House of Industry' was a very apt one, as was the latter day description of 'Workhouse'.

The emphasis on work is underlined by the range of buildings once in use – stables, a barn, carpenter's and shoemaker's shops, spinning and weaving rooms, dairy, brewhouse, bakery, washhouse, starching room, hemp warehouse, kitchens and office. Interestingly, when Lady Proctor visited the town in 1764, she recorded that spinning was the chief trade carried on and one wonders whether this was due to the output from the 'House of Industry'.

Shoes for inmates were a continuing expense even if they cost only between ¹/₂d and 3¹/₂d in the 1780s. Such prices are, perhaps, put into perspective by the knowledge that 3lb of butter cost 1s 10¹/₂d, cheese was 4¹/₂d per pound while 3¹/₂lb of soap could be bought for 2s.

While there is evidence that the local Guardians were, on the whole, a kindly set of men they, like the Justices, had a duty to avoid any unnecessary expense falling on the local rates. This is why poor children were indentured to traders and private houses; why, in 1844, the Churchwardens and Overseers borrowed £40 to send a young labourer and his wife to Australia, and two young women and their four children to Canada; and why, in earlier times, unmarried mothers were subjected to public examination in order to ascertain the names of the fathers of their children, so that both, but principally the father, could be ordered to pay for the child's keep.

That the Churchwardens and Overseers were not always so harsh is borne out by many entries in the Churchwarden's Book which Radford quotes in his book, and which throw an interesting light on life in the town. In 1712, for example, they gave money 'severrel times to disabled shoulders' (men wounded in the war in the Netherlands); in 1723 money went to 'shippbroken men' and in 1726 to 'Sailors yt had been Slaves in Turkey'. In 1764 they gave a shilling to '2 Soldiers widows with children' and in 1779 they paid 'for a new pipe for Ingens' (the town fire engine). One surprising section contains details of payments for the killing of what were obviously regarded as unwelcome pests of field and garden. This war against nature lasted through the whole of the 1700s. Typical entries include payment of 1s for 'killing a Fox in the Townfields' and 4d for '4 Moles catchd in the Church Yard', plus many other payments for sparrows at 3d a dozen and hedgehogs at 4d a head. No doubt a very welcome source of additional income for men and boys of the town.

When times were hard those two essentials, bread and fuel, were often absent from many poor homes in the town. So it was that those who were able to donated money to help the poor and needy. In Holt Stephen Feake, in 1661, together with two anonymous donors, gave yearly rent values together worth £2 10s 0d. In 1738 Blanch Schuldham bequeathed £50 to yield £2 10s 0d a year for the purchase of bread for the poor, to be given out in the form of two dozen penny loaves every other Sunday. Rev Joshua Smith, Rector of Holt, bequeathed £200 for the same purpose and this was invested in Government Stock in 1848 to produce £6 6s 0d per annum, less income tax. Finally, Mr Wallace Mallett, on the day that he died, 4th June 1852, bequeathed £200 with the interest also to be used to provide bread for the poor and needy.

The six charities were eventually combined and were administered by the Parish Council until April 1958 when they were passed to a group of Trustees, a balance of £46 being handed over to them. By this time the money was being used to provide not just bread but fuel as well and evidence that this had long been the practice is borne out by entries in the 'Coal Book' of 1850. Nowadays the total income is in the region of £12 a year and instead of gifts of bread and fuel cash grants of £5 to £10 are given to those in need as and when necessary.

In medieval days church guilds provided much needed comfort and help and in Holt it was the Guild of St Mary, the altar of St Mary the Virgin in the south aisle of the parish church being largely maintained by it. The Guild was in effect a benefit society, a burial club, a mutual improvement society, perhaps an early form of trade union, and an organiser of festivals and entertainment in the Guild House in the town. It was suppressed at the time of the Reformation but some of its aims were taken up by the Holt Provident Society, formed in June 1794. The rules and regulations of the Society provided for members to pay a monthly fee of 3s 6d, the money to be put into a box which had three locks – and three different keyholders! No member could benefit until he had belonged to the Society for five years. Then his widow was entitled to £20 per year or, if there were children, £10 for her and £10 for the children. Weekly sums could also be paid to help members who became destitute.

Education

Although it was the weekly market – originally held on Tuesdays, then Saturdays, then Wednesdays and, finally, every Friday – which established Holt as a thriving town, much of its development and prosperity has been due to the founding and growth of Gresham's School.

The Gresham family originated from the nearby village of the same name, moving into the Manor House in Holt during the 15th century. Sir John Gresham, one time financial agent of Cardinal Wolsey and Thomas Cromwell, Lord

The pre-1858 building of Gresham's School

Mayor, Sheriff and Alderman of the City of London and member of the Mercers' Company, gained much from the redistribution of monastic lands. He was given that part of Beeston Regis priory lands that included the Manors of Holt Hales and Holt Perers. Having decided to found a school, he bought the Perers Manor House – 'a substantial and commodious property' – from his brother William. With the Mercers' Company already having its own school and also being a member of the Worshipful Company of Fishmongers, he signed over the building to the latter endowing it in 1554 with both Manors, various pieces of land in Norfolk and freehold property in Cripplegate in London. Tragically, he died of the plague a week later and so did not see his dream fulfilled. The school officially opened in 1562 to provide education for 30 free scholars, plus boarders and day boys, but early records were lost in the Great Fire of London in 1666. Academic standards and progress were apparently good and early associations were forged with Sydney Sussex and Caius Colleges in Cambridge.

All the early headmasters, right through to 1729, were practising clergymen, although this did not necessarily imply particularly high standards on their part. Thomas Tallis, headmaster from 1606 to 1640, was an exception and his contribution to the development of the school is remembered in the House that carries his name. Rev Thomas Cooper, Rector of Little Barningham and appointed as Usher to the School, was dismissed in 1632 for non-attendance and later hanged on Christmas Day at Norwich for his part in the Royalist rebellion of 1650 which, incidentally, found several supporters in the town. Henry Mazey (1660–1665), later to become headmaster of Norwich Grammar School, was obviously some-

thing of a disciplinarian, for in later years the boys at Norwich petitioned the Mayor of the City asking for his removal. Rev Thomas Atkins (1787–1809) was dismissed and Rev Benjamin Pullan (1809–1858), Vicar of Weybourne, taught boys by repetition – and beat them if they got it wrong. This approach was also adopted by Charles Elton, a savage disciplinarian who beat the boys unmercifully and who was one of the last of the old order, resigning in 1867.

In 1858 the old schoolhouse was demolished and the present buildings erected facing the market place. By 1900 the school was acknowledged to be the wealthiest educational charity in the country and the opportunity was taken to completely reorganize the curriculum and methods of teaching. The existing staff were pensioned off and George William Saul Howson was appointed headmaster with a supporting staff of four. The number of free places, originally set at 30, had been increased to 50 by 1821 but dwindled to two after 1900. The school introduced the 'honour' system to maintain discipline; this required every boy not to tell lies or indulge in 'any unclean practice', to own up to any misdeeds and either admonish, or inform on, others. The system continued into the mid-1930s, but many old boys, including W. H. Auden and Benjamin Britten, disliked it, saying it gave them a guilt complex.

By now, too, the emphasis was away from subjects such as Greek and Latin and more orientated to the sciences. The amphitheatre was built; Old School House opened as a junior boarding house in 1903; Woodlands, once a private house, became part of the school and Farfield was added in 1911. About this time, work began on the Chapel, despite an engineer's warning that it was on the site of an underground stream. Howson died in 1919 and was buried by the side of his Chapel.

During the Second World War the school was requisitioned for use as a barracks, and tanks practised in the grounds; the boys were removed to two hotels in Newquay. The first post-war headmaster was Martin John Olivier, cousin of the actor, and in 1955 Logie Bruce Lockhart was appointed. During his term, until his retirement in 1982, the new houses of Kenwyn and Tallis were opened, the first girl pupils were accepted, the Reith Block came into use (Lord Reith being an old boy), the swimming pool was opened, a new dining hall, administrative block and sanatorium were provided, academic standards increased and plans were put under way for the introduction of computer studies. The school's continual educational expansion programme is reflected in the building of the Cairns Centre dedicated to providing the best teaching in art and design.

Nowadays, when school breaks up for the holidays the boys and girls simply depart by car and coach. During the early 18th century such an occasion was marked by a party at the White Lion for parents, local gentry and tradesmen, with the pupils providing a play, mostly in Greek, Latin and French. Towards the end of the century the venue was changed to the Feathers Hotel.

The great fire: 1708

The old school house, apart from a charred gable, survived the fire of 1708, one of the few in the town centre to do so. It must have been quite a conflagration, for the Royal Brief of 1723 described it as a 'sudden and lamentable fire at Holt-Market aforesaid, which in the Space of Three Hours burnt down to the ground almost the whole Town and the Parish Church standing therein, which was then a well-built Fabrick, kept in good repair, and consisted of three large Isles covered with lead'.

How the fire started nobody knows but its swiftness and ferocity can be judged by the fact that the butchers did not have time to move the meat off their stalls. The thatched roof over the church chancel caught alight and the heat and flames melted the lead roof which fell in a molten state onto the floor and walls, cracking and ruining them. Flames also funnelled up the steeple – a reputed landmark for ships – and burnt the frames holding the two bells, which crashed down into the body of the church.

Total damage was estimated at £11,258, a lot of money in those days, and while neighbouring towns and villages were quick to help – North Walsham sent £32 13s 6d within a week; Hingham's contribution was £10 11s 0d and Pulham St Mary sent 3s 3½d – it took several years for the town to recover. The rebuilding of the church was not completed until 1727 when pews were apportioned. The men were to sit to the north of the aisle, the women to the south while 'ye Scole

Boyes [from Gresham's], ye Aprentices and ye Charity Children' found themselves in the gallery which ran across the tower arch. Many notable people contributed to the rebuilding and refurbishing of the church. Among them were the Prime Minister (and local squire) Sir Robert Walpole, who gave £50 and a silver plate, the Secretary of State, Charles, Lord Townshend gave the same and George, Prince of Wales, donated £100 and a large silver flagon. The rebuilding work cost £1,229 and local craftsmen were responsible for much of the work; the old spire was not replaced.

Following the fire the heart of the town was virtually rebuilt. Previously it had clustered round the church but the new centre was where we see it today with the broad expanse of the market place being reduced by the row of properties which forms the division between it and Bull Street. The line of properties on the southern side comprising the Feathers Hotel and C. T. Baker Limited was retained. The latter dates from 1631 and the fire left the gable walls intact. When the shop front was rebuilt in 1981 part of an original beam, complete with charred end where it went into the western gable, was found as were wooden dowels used in the roof, hand-made nails and 17th-century red bricks.

The Feathers Hotel was rebuilt in 1709 and in 1790 was described as one of the principal inns (the other being the White Lion); in its time has served as the town's post office, venue for Excise meetings, and a meeting place where the gentry received their land taxes. During the 19th century it housed an inland revenue office; Barclays Bank hired a room as temporary bank and office; Petty Sessions were held there; and after the closure of the Corn Hall merchants met to inspect samples displayed on the pavement outside. Not that it has always been regarded as the best in town: in 1772, Lady Beauchamp Proctor, in a letter to her sister, said that the Feathers was 'a most wretched inn, we had much ado to get a dinner, a rotten leg of mutton which all this miserable place afforded, and a piece of beef that had died in a ditch. Yet the town is not small and is really a pretty one.' The hotel also received something of a back handed compliment in

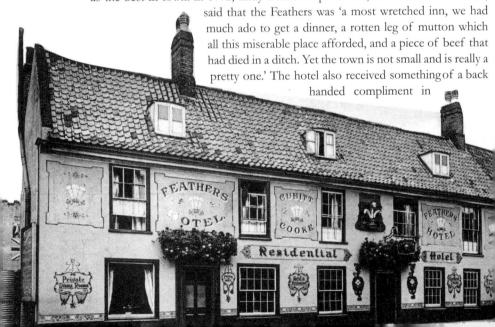

Larner's (and, just beyond it, Baker's) in 1910

April 1869 when James Hooper, writing in the *Eastern Daily Press,* recorded that the Feathers was 'a place which seems so flourishing that casual wayfarers will find the atmosphere oppressive'. Today wayfarers will find it one of the best establishments in the area.

With the rebuilding of the town went a desire for better fire protection, something underlined by an entry in the minutes of the Fishmongers' Company of 9th December 1763. The town wanted its own fire engine but could not afford the cost of £60. Edward Astley of Melton Constable Hall generously donated £20 and, because the townspeople still could not afford the balance, they petitioned the Company who gave another £20 towards the cost. Insuring against loss from fire was also growing in popularity and the fire plaque of the Norwich Union Insurance Society over the front door of Hanworth House in Bull Street – built in 1744 – is a reminder of those days.

In those days the 'engine' would have been pulled by hand but later by horses that were grazed on the Spout Hills. Prior to 1936 the engine was kept in the old mortuary adjoining the Pound on Obelisk Plain. It then moved into the fire station established in the Shirehall, in that part now occupied by the Nationwide Building Society. Bill Taberham has recalled the horse-drawn appliance with its hand operated pump and the fact that if the fire was in the town centre it was quicker to hand-haul it to the scene rather than try and catch the horses on Spout Hills first! The summoning bell was on the adjoining water tower. The story is told of the man from Edgefield whose house was on fire who dashed into Holt, furiously rang the bell and then dashed home again without waiting to give anyone his name and address. When the firemen arrived at the station they did not know where to go and this was one fire that went unattended!

The Shirehall was reconstructed after the fire of 1708, although a massive internal supporting post on a stone base, and original basement walls, survive from medieval days. There is thought to have been a second supporting post and it is suggested that the stone outside the front door, long used as a mounting stone, was the supporting base; it would appear to have the same cut and pattern on its underside as the stone inside. In earlier times the building was a corn market house where officials collected tolls and imposed fines for breaches of early weights and measures standards. It has seen the holding of the Quarter Sessions and for 130 years, ending in March 1975, magistrates met there in Petty Session.

Some of the most interesting glimpses into local life during the late 18th and early 19th centuries are to be found in Mary Hardy's Diaries, published by the Norfolk Record Society and extracts from which are quoted by Mr Basil Cozens-Hardy in his book *The Story of Letheringsett*. On 22nd May 1786 she refers to a 'new

The water tower (last used in 1955), Shire Hall Plain. The Shirehall itself (on the right of the picture) was modernised in 1935 to be used as a general meeting place, parish council chamber, magistrates' court and working men's club; it now houses the Body and Face Place beauty salon.

mill' at Holt and 26th November the following year sees her attending a horse fair in Holt, an occasion repeated on 25th April 1788 when the Holt Stage Coach was sold for £7 7s 0d. On 23rd April 1789 Mary records celebrations in the area to mark the King's recovery 'from his late state of insanity'; 500 people dined in Holt Market Place on plum puddings and boiled beef and there was a dance at the Shirehall in the evening. She also refers to the Black Boys public house 'adjoining' the Shirehall, and strikes a more serious note in a reference, in December 1800, to local riots against the high price of food, especially flour.

Fears of a French invasion led to a meeting at Holt Shirehall on 3rd May 1794 'for raising volunteers by subscription for the defence of the country', and in June the following year she records two regiments of artillery passing through the town on their way to Weybourne. An intriguing entry for 3rd June 1795 records that 'Thos Reynolds let himself as a substitute for 16 guineas' and this is followed on 19th October by 'Wm rid to Sheringham in the morning for Mr Page to come and swear in Wm's substitute. Mr Jodrell came in after service and swore in the man.'

A later group of Holt volunteers: the year is 1900.

This anticipation of invasion led to the raising of a volunteer force and Holt and district contributed 120 men, many of these being 'balloted' at local meetings. Joseph Baker was one who was balloted but, as we have seen above, according to the custom at the time, he was able to provide 'an able and sufficient person to serve as his substitute, which said substitute has been duly sworn enrolled and approved'. By taking the place of another man the substitute not only received half the volunteer's payment (£20), but his wife and family were assured of relief, paid by the parish and reimbursed by the county of the regiment in which he served. In the case of one Ann Jackson she received 6s a week for herself and three young sons while her husband served as a corporal in the Royal Pembroke Fusilier Battalion.

Some Norfolk parishes were fined for not providing sufficient men. The Churchwardens and Overseers of the Poor in Holt were fined £20 in error and they successfully recovered this sum in November 1809. Mary Hardy was able to record on 8th November 1803 that 'The Holt and Letheringsett Volunteers were reviewed this aft. by a General. The Rainham Rangers and Fakenham Volunteers were sent to Yarmouth to guard the coast.' She makes no mention of Nelson, but the house that bears his name in White Lion Street was once occupied by a Mrs Suckling, an aunt, and it is known he visited her several times. A bellarmine dug up in the garden was possibly brought back by him from a foreign voyage.

Recreation and leisure

One aspect of town life that has diminished in importance is the enjoyment of open spaces for recreation and leisure purposes. True, the Country Park with its 100 acres was opened in April 1980 at a cost of some £54,000, but to older residents it is a poor substitute for what went before.

Prior to the Inclosure Acts commons and heaths were quite extensive, the heath area offering not just pleasant walks but a racecourse and a bathing pool, the latter existing in a primitive form until the last war when it became contaminated by phosphorous. After the inclosures 120 acres were allocated to the poor of the parish so that they could collect fuel and cut turf, and racing transferred to Swaffham where the course was reputed to be equal, if not superior, after Newmarket, to most courses in England. At Holt races to the value of 20 and 30 guineas were competed for by jockeys and local gentry and meetings were usually accompanied by cock-fights and glittering Assemblies in the Shirehall.

Spout Hills have always been a popular open space and today are managed by the Town Council as part of the countryside stewardship scheme. Preston's *Almanack* of 1883 refers to a stream 'unceasing and unchangeable in volume, flowing at the rate of 60 barrels an hour; the water as might be expected from so wonderful a natural filter as the gravel of the hill is of exceptional purity and softness, in consequence of its inherent properties a large and thriving Mineral Water Business has been formed. A scheme for utilising this natural boon and efficiently draining the town has been projected.'

Spout Hills

An earlier report, in 1864, had quoted a yield of 25 gallons a minute at the Spout itself and 38 gallons a minute at Mr Brumell's garden after the addition of 'the other small springs at the Spouts Hill'. Allowing 10 gallons of water per head 'including the watering of roads, flushing drains etc', it was estimated that the town would need 16,000 gallons a day. This would involve the provision of hydraulic rams, a length of open stream and then iron pipes to carry the water to a water tower on Shirehall Plain; this survived until demolition in 1957. It was further recommended that a horse and man be hired to drive an extra pump to supply any extra water required to meet public demand. Also that six hydrants be fixed in 'the most prominent positions in case of fire' and that 'a few public taps might be fixed for the poor but these should be made self-acting to prevent waste'. And all this to be carried out at an estimated cost of £1175! Parts of two of the old taps still survive, one on the gable end of a cottage at the top of Letheringsett Hill and one at the entrance to Weston Square.

Now no longer used, this water supply served the town well. Some residents can still recall the practice of the Misses Outlaw, during their time at the King's Head, of dispatching the ostler every day to the Spout to bring back a jug of spring water to stand on the bar-top for use by customers.

But it was not just for water that people went to Spout Hills. Both children and adults washed their clothes in the spring and hung the garments to dry on the gorse bushes, which dotted the hillside. And they have also been the scene for many town celebrations, including Peace Festivals of 1814 and 1919, Queen Victoria's Jubilee in June 1887, the Coronation of King George V and Queen Mary in June 1911 and on Coronation Day 1953.

Victorian Holt

The 1831 Census recorded 306 houses inhabited by 327 families, with 12 properties uninhabited and six in course of construction. Of the families 99 were employed in agriculture and 160 in trade or manufacture. The population of 1,622 comprised 790 males and 832 females.

Victoria's reign saw many changes in the town. By the time of her coronation in 1838 the population had increased to nearly 1,700 and Wesleyan, Primitive Methodists and the Society of Friends were all well established, although few of the latter sect were actually living in the town.

The National School met in the Shirehall, having been established in January 1835 by public subscription. It did not move into its own premises until 1843. White's Norfolk *Directory* for 1836 records six attorneys, six Fire and Life Officers, eight innkeepers, 12 boot and shoe makers, three brewers, two glovers, five grocers and drapers, three hairdressers, three ironmongers, 11 joiners and wheelwrights, three milliners, two surgeons, five tailors and drapers and three watchmakers among the population.

Coach transport continued into the beginning of the 1900s. This is Ben Empson and friends outside his home in New Street in 1912.

The town was well served by coaches, the Norfolk Regulator leaving the Feathers every Monday, Wednesday and Friday morning at 5.15 to London via Dereham, Newmarket and Cambridge while other services took passengers and goods to Norwich, Blakeney, Cley, King's Lynn, Fakenham and Cromer. A post office is recorded in the High Street in 1846, the post box closing at 4pm 'but letters can be posted up to 4.15 by payment of 1d extra and 2d extra up to 20 minutes past 4'. James Crowe was in business as a carrier from his house in Norwich Road to Blakeney, Cley, Langham and Norwich, while Mr Howes and Samuel Mason left respectively from the King's Head and Angel to Cromer and King's Lynn.

By 1854 the population had increased very slowly to 1,726 (835 males and 891 females), all living in 368 properties (an average of 4.5 per property compared with the modern average of 2.5); there were 26 uninhabited houses and three in course of construction. The streets were 'well paved and lighted from the gas works erected in 1841' and selling gas at 9s 1d per 1000 cubic feet; a new police station (Hempstead Road) was 'about to be erected'. The British School in Withers Street (now New Street) had been built in 1851 at the expense of William Cozens Hardy of Letheringsett and this also doubled as a public meeting place and a Sunday place of worship for the Wesleyan Reformers. When the southern end of New Street was constructed it provided a new through highway, joining up with the existing Withers Street, which connected Cley Road and Cross Street.

The Literary Society had moved into its premises in New Street (now Barclays

Bank car park) and with a library of 'more than 2000 volumes' was providing a very useful service.

In March 1855 one of Holt's most famous sons and characters was presented to Queen Victoria at Brompton Barracks. He was James Olley and during service in the 4th Light Dragoons he took part in the charge of the Light Brigade in which he was wounded five times and lost the sight of his left eye. By 1888 he was unemployed but was championed by Mr H. M. Robinson of Knapton Hall, and the *Dereham and Fakenham Times* opened a fund which raised enough money to set him up in business as a horse breaker and trainer. His stables were on the site of the present County Library in Church Street and he lived in a beerhouse in Bull Street known then as 'The Stores' and now as the Cottage Boutique. Could the occasional 'presence' experienced in the cellar be the spirit of James visiting his old home? He later moved to Blakeney and Salthouse and eventually died in 1920 at Balaclava Cottage at Elsing and now lies in an unmarked grave. He was known affectionately as 'Old Balaclava', was married three times, always proudly wore his medals and reputedly never returned from Aldborough Fair 'without a black eye or two'.

The parish church was thoroughly restored in 1863. The previous year had seen the building of the Gothic-style Methodist Church on Obelisk Plain, said to be the best of its kind in the country, although others were critical of

its 'streaky bacon' brickwork and its 'vast and cold' interior. At least it survived the Primitive and Wesleyan Methodist churches, although the former remains converted to residential accommodation facing Albert Street. Gone, too, is the Quaker Meeting House, formerly sited to the rear of the present post office and well established by 1678 with its own burial ground and minister.

The arrival of the railway on 1st October 1884, as an extension of the Eastern and Midland line to Melton Constable, had great implications for the town. The days of the carriers were passing. Milk trains carried their loads of 17-gallon churns to Finsbury Park. The weekly cattle market received a

Holt Post Office c.1930

A well attended Methodist service, probably a special children's service.

Obelisk Plain in the 1880s.

boost as upwards of 25 cattle wagons (with 8–10 cattle in each) brought and took away their loads, with herds of animals being driven along Hempstead Road and through the Market Place – not to mention the occasional runaway horse to add to the excitement. As one resident has recalled, 'We hardly dared go down the street when they were clearing the sale yard'.

Mr William Gardner, one of six clerks employed at the station in the 1920s, recalled the 1,000 or so wagons of sugar beet handled every season, the 20,000 grain sacks hired out every month during the winter and the specially converted wagons bringing in household refuse from Sheringham to the branch line to Kelling Heath tip. He also remembered the troop and ammunition trains passing through to Weybourne as the camp established itself, and the popularity of the excursion trains, in their distinctive 'golden gorse' livery; they took locals to such places as Birmingham, Manchester and London (King's Cross) and brought in day trippers to Cromer and Sheringham from various places in the Midlands. Gresham's School brought in extra business, too, as parents came to see their children, and trunks and cases had to be moved in and out at the beginning and end of every term.

Although this was a time of change for Holt it took place without really altering the character of the town. The Obelisk Plain was much the same as it is today, except for the village pump and horse trough. Tom Loynes was in business as a blacksmith in the yard behind King's and Barnham's shop. He is remembered for the fact that following an accident with hot metal which damaged the nerves of his eyelids he had to physically hold up the lids in order to see ahead; part of his craftsmanship still exists over the yard entrance.

Following the harvests, men would call from door to door offering rabbits for sale at 10d each. Concerts could be enjoyed in the Concert Hall in New Street. Coal was coming in by train and being sold at £8 a ton and for young-sters the smell of newly baked bread was always an attraction. They would stand on the pavement at Shirehall Plain and look down into the cellar bakery under what is now Paige's shop and restaurant watching the bread being taken out of the ovens and enjoying what Mrs Ransome remembered as 'that lovely smell'. The Elizabethan cellar retains much of its original character. During restoration of this 17th-century building some small beautiful original windows were uncovered on the front elevation and have been restored.

For amusements there were concerts by travelling groups and Punch and Judy men, the occasional dancing bear, German bands, barrel-organs and accompany-

Holt Board School 1902, with headmaster F. T. Hutchens

ing monkeys, horse fairs, sales and circuses on The Fairstead and off Hempstead Road, and, of course, the open areas of the Lowes and Spout Hills for games and walks. Not that there would have been many of these in April 1919, when the snow was so deep that sheep could not be driven from Kelling to the market.

The Mutual Improvement Society was meeting at the Shirehall, and the water cart was a regular sight as it passed laying the dust of the unmade roads. The cinema was also a great attraction. This was, at various times, in a tent on the Mill Meadow (now 'Millcourt' housing complex) and in a corrugated iron building in a yard behind the site of the new shops at Poundhouse where, the late Mr Archie Checkley recalled, you had to be prepared to move around during wet weather in order to keep dry! Then it was in the old Co-op hall (now flats) in New Street. The Regal Cinema in Peacock Lane opened on 8th March 1937 and closed in 1962, re-opening as a Bingo Hall. For the more energetic there was the town Football Club, opposite the Holt Garage on the Cromer Road, although a canvas screen was erected alongside the road to prevent too many free spectators.

The drinking man had a choice of ten pubs for, in addition to the remaining Feathers, King's Head and Railway Tavern, there were the Queen Adelaide in New Street (now flats); the Carpenters Arms in Norwich Road (now a private house); the Angel (formerly on the site of the present Post Office); the Star on Fish Hill (now an antique shop and formerly known as the Dolphin); the Bull in Bull Street (now a baker's/delicatessen) and the Paul Pry in Albert Street (now a private house). The latest to close, the White Lion, has been converted into shops and flats. During the late 1800s the Red Lion in New Street was a favourite haunt of the men working in the rope factory in what is now known as Fairstead Row. For the more temperate the Rose Tea Gardens on the corner of Cromer and Kelling roads offered afternoon tea and the opportunity of wandering round the gardens; it closed during the 1930s.

Whether it was the influence of Gresham's or not, Holt certainly did well for schools. During the 1920s and 1930s there were, in addition to the Board School (now Dyson and Faircloth's garage in New Street, but serving as an ARP centre and egg packing station after closing as a school), and the National School in Norwich Road (now demolished), five private schools in the town. All of the latter have now disappeared and have been converted into private homes, although Miss Preston's old, wooden schoolroom remains in Hempstead Road.

Worshippers were welcome at the parish church and the Methodist church on Obelisk Plain; the Plymouth Brethren met at the top of Letheringsett Hill, the Wesleyans in what is now St John's Hall and the Salvation Army on Saturday nights in Oddfellows Hall. The latter was built in 1839 as a Calvinist church and sold in 1857 to become a corn exchange – indeed, the O. S. map of 1887 refers to what is now Albert Street as 'Corn Hall Street'. It then served as a concert hall and an ex-servicemen's club before adopting its new title in the early 1900s. It was sold in 1981 to become an auction hall, and is now an antique centre. The old burial ground in Albert Street has been converted into a quiet amenity area with seats and is known as the Methodist Memorial Garden.

The Holt Discharged Soldiers and Sailors Allotment Association Limited was

Unveiling and dedication of the war memorial by Commander Douglas King, Sunday 29th May 1921

The market place in 1908: bank and Caxton printing works on the left, 'Blind Sam' centre foreground

formed on 4th October 1920 to run allotments formerly owned by the British Legion on land once owned by Holt Hall and members met at the Ivy Leaf Club in Albert Street; today there are some 77 members.

Prior to the unveiling of the War Memorial by the Bishop of Thetford on Sunday 29th May 1921 its site was occupied by the now restored Jubilee Memorial standing on Obelisk Plain. When in the Market Place it provided a much needed gas light, although it was affectionately known as 'Blind Sam' because it was more often out than providing illumination. The Obelisk itself started life as one of a pair of gateposts at the entrance to Melton Park although no one appears to know when it came to Holt.

The British Legion homes in Cley Road were opened in March 1929 by the Earl of Leicester. On 1st November the same year the R101 was seen over Holt during a trial flight. Holt mill, built in 1795, had its sails removed in 1925 and was dismantled in 1974.

The new Post Office, built at a cost of £4,500, was opened on 23rd August 1934 by Lady Cozens Hardy and for those who possessed wirelesses October 1936 was an important month for this was when the town received international mention as local boy 'Yodelling' Reggie Fuller appeared on Radio Luxembourg as one of Carrol Levis' 'Discoveries'. Many local people were also to find temporary stardom some 34 years later, in 1970, as 'extras' in the film *The Go-Between* which was filmed in the area. Mr Charles Winn was the gardener – an appropriate choice for one so long in the business of horticulture, floristry and market gardening!

Electricity arrived in 1931, just 90 years after the first 14 street gas lamps were provided. Appropriately, C. T. Baker's, the town's oldest business (established 1770), was the first to install this new fangled system of lighting.

The Working Men's Club, established in 1878 and meeting at the Shirehall, closed in 1935 after offering 'papers, books, games such as bagatelle, dominoes and chess etc which afford both pleasant and profitable recreation for the working classes of Holt'. Among the rules there were offences for swearing, abusive language, spitting and throwing orange peel about, and no one was allowed to read a newspaper for more than ten minutes at a time.

An example of the sense of community that existed in the town has been remembered by the late Mr 'Bumps' Caston. He recalled that when Mr George Larner lay dying in a room above his shop the Market Place was strawed to about a foot deep to deaden the sound from the new buses which were then beginning to pass through the town.

Holt Hall, built in the Gothic style in 1846 by Mr W. H. Pemberton and extended in 1864, was sold to Norfolk County Council in 1947 for use as a residential school. It has, so far, managed to survive a series of budget cuts in the Council's educational expenditure.

The Literary Institute, opened in 1854, closed in 1955 and was demolished some eight years later to make way for the new branch of Barclays Bank; because of complaints from lady members in 1913 smoking was banned during whist drives and then completely until after 6pm.

Holt Hall in 1907

A sale at the Holt sale yard in August 1952, in aid of the Lynmouth flood disaster.

End of an era

The end of Holt as a market town came in 1960 when Irelands, who had run the market for many years, finally closed it down. From its heyday, when hundreds of cattle would pass through in a single day, to its war-time spell as a Ministry of Food Grading Centre, when 300 and more cattle were graded and dispatched to Islington and the Midlands for slaughter, and later as an open market where pigs and poultry and general merchandise dominated the scene, it had come a long way since the street market of medieval days.

The night of 19th August 1968 was both an exciting and a tragic one for the town. At 10pm two RAF aircraft – a Victor tanker from RAF Marham and a Canberra from RAF Bruggen in Germany – collided over the town killing seven RAF men and giving many residents a narrow escape from death as pieces of the two aircraft hurtled down, the largest piece falling in Gravel Pit Lane. A memorial to the men was unveiled in St Andrew's church on Sunday 20th August 2000.

On a literally brighter note this month also saw the introduction of the 'Brighter Holt' scheme. Sponsored by the Chamber of Trade, it aimed to emulate the famous Magdalen Street scheme in Norwich with owners of properties choosing from 18 approved colours, mostly pastel 'but with one or two varied hues to set off buildings needing special emphasis'. The Parish Council erected elegant street lamps and it was subsequently reported that only one or two property owners declined to decorate and renovate their properties. Holt was the first small market town in the county, and the third in the country, to introduce such a scheme.

The year 1965 saw the formation of the Holt Society, a band of people dedicated to preserving all that is best in the town. Their efforts received a terrific boost in December 1974 when the whole of the town centre was designated a Conservation Area. They keep a close eye on all planning applications, have published a town walks leaflet and would like to see the establishment of a town museum, an aim shared by the Holt History Group founded in 1986 and currently with some 140 members. The group is interested in all aspects of local and general Norfolk life.

The following year saw the formation of the Holt and Neighbourhood Housing Society Limited, with the aim of preserving the character of the built environment for local people. The Society owns 33 properties in the town and surrounding area, including 17th-century cottages in Carpenters Arms Yard and the Victorian Lees Terrace. Future acquisitions are planned and donations are always welcome to help continue this valuable work.

17th September 1969 was a sad day for many local people, for it saw the loss of one of the town's most beautiful landmarks, a 100-year-old chestnut tree on Star Plain, a victim of old age and in a dangerous condition.

Public interest in the future of the town was also demonstrated in September 1973 when so many people turned up for a public meeting due to be held at the Shirehall that it had to be moved to Gresham's School. Among the proposals discussed was the possible doubling of the town's population to 6,000; the provision of a by-pass; the building of a new Middle School and possibly two others

Lee's Yard – now converted and known as Lyle's Yard.

on the northern outskirts of the town; pedestrianisation of the Market Place; the provision of additional car parks and a ban on industrial development. The Holt Society opposed proposals for increasing the population to such an extent although the Chamber of Trade would have liked to see more people coming into the town, some industry and the provision of a new school. To those who argued that a by-pass would split the town it was pointed out that this was already happening with the railway line.

The long awaited Community Centre was opened on 8th March 1975 by the Lord Lieutenant of Norfolk, Lt Col Sir Edmund Bacon, the site having been given by the former Erpingham Rural District Council and the raising of well over £19,000 locally toward the total cost of £66,000.

A town sign was presented to the community in June 1976 by the two local Women's Institutes and depicted Sir Gordon Gresham and Lady Alice Perers and was one of many pieces of craftsmanship by Harry Carter which can be seen all over the county. It was surmounted by the ubiquitous Holt owl, the symbol of the town and originating from the apocryphal tale of the locals who captured such a bird and put it in the Pound, only to be surprised when they found it gone in the morning! Like the owl, the Pound has long since gone but it served for many years on a piece of land adjacent to the southern boundary wall of the Methodist Church on Obelisk Plain. The town sign was replaced in 1990 with one recalling the legend of the Holt owl.

Delivering the goods – Byford's cart

The year 1980 saw civilisation really arriving with the opening of the new (improved) £1 million sewage works serving 3,083 people in Holt and Letheringsett and with a design capacity for a population of 5,000 people. The population of Holt in 1999 was 3,845.

The following year was a notable one for the town when it won the title of Best Kept Market Town. This success was repeated in various forms in later years – Best Kept Village Competition in 1997, the Anglia in Bloom Competition for Small Market Towns in 1992, 1993, 1995 and 1996 and 1998 (Runner Up in 1994) and as a finalist in the Britain in Bloom Competition in 1993 and 1996.

In August 1991 work started on the £1m one-and-three-quarter-mile by-pass which, although generating many objections at the time, has proved to have been the catalyst which has led to Holt being the attractive and thriving town it is today.

Attempts to establish a small market on a site to the rear of the Feathers Hotel proved unsuccessful and today this has been developed as a small shopping complex.

Budgens supermarket arrived on 3rd December 1985, bringing with it some much needed extra parking spaces; the Appleyard and nearby Old Stables Yard have brought new shopping areas into the town centre. The attractive Methodist Memorial Garden in Albert Street is a peaceful haven and has proved popular with both residents and visitors since it opened on 23rd April 1992. The Millen-

Delivering the goods – butcher's vans

Holt market place c.1916

nium Shelter in the Market Place provides a comfortable seat from which to watch the world go by.

The North Norfolk Local Plan has designated the town centre as a Conservation Area. The town is surrounded by areas of land that are either in an Area of Outstanding Natural Beauty or of High Landscape Value. With the exception of the building site to the south of the by-pass between the playing field and the industrial area there is no scope for further estate building; any future need will, therefore, have to be met from infilling as sites become available. As at June 2000 there were 14 dwellings under construction and a further 118 with either outline or detailed planning permission awaiting construction. With limited expansion possible on the industrial estate off Hempstead Road the demographic nature of the town is unlikely to change. A site for a new Youth Club has been identified and an ambitious project to research and record the lives of those listed on the war memorial has been completed and a commemorative book is kept in the church.

So what of the future? Whilst there is the possibility for some limited growth over the next few years Holt has really expanded and developed to its practical limits. Future efforts will have to be directed to making the town an even more attractive shopping and residential centre than it already is. It appears to be generally agreed that a new traffic management scheme is desirable but progress here will only come with funding being made available. The Chamber of Trade would also like to see a better, and brighter, lighting scheme, accompanied by a town-wide effort to improve the overall appearance of the town by bringing back the styles and colours of the Georgian period – something already achieved in the decoration of the Owl Tea Rooms and Bakery. Reference has already been made to the 'Brighter Holt' scheme of the 1960s; now is the time for something similar for the new Millennium. Advice is available from the Conservation and Design Section of North Norfolk District Council.

Holt is no longer a market town. It is an attractive residential and shopping town and has the potential to build on its present popularity.

ADVANCED MODELLING IN
N GAUGE

ADVANCED MODELLING IN
N GAUGE

NOEL LEAVER

☒ THE CROWOOD PRESS

First published in 2021 by
The Crowood Press Ltd
Ramsbury, Marlborough
Wiltshire SN8 2HR

enquiries@crowood.com

www.crowood.com

British Library Cataloguing-in-Publication Data
A catalogue record for this book is available from the British Library.

ISBN 978 1 78500 945 7

Acknowledgements
Thanks are due to the many people who have helped me with this book: Julian Thornhill and
Alison McGregor for proof reading; Grahame Hedges, who has made valuable contributions
and allowed me to use many of his photographs; Richard Bardsley, who suggested I write it;
the many members of the N-gauge group at Farnham and District Model Railway Club who
have helped; the builders of the different layouts pictured; and to everyone who has given
me permission to use pictures they have taken, particularly Tony Wright and Chris Nevard
for their photographs of Wickwar.

Frontispiece: Rhosteigne was built by Keith Robbins, and is now owned by Nick Beischer,
who has developed it further. The impressive scratch-built LMS signal box sets the location.
The passing Farish A1 Pacific shows the level of detail of modern N-gauge models.

Typeset by Simon and Sons

Cover design by Blue Sunflower Creative

Printed and bound in India by Parksons Graphics Pvt. Ltd., Mumbai.

CONTENTS

Stoney Lane Depot by Grahame Hedges recreates a small area of South London around 1990, showing how you can create a complex urban scene in a small area. The scenic part is about 7 × 2ft (2 × 0.6m). It showcases Grahame's scratch-built buildings.

INTRODUCTION

This book assumes you are already familiar with the basics of N-gauge modelling; if not, *Making a Start in N Gauge* by Richard Bardsley (Crowood) is an excellent introduction to the subject. I hope to be able to extend your skills: to build more from scratch; to be more ambitious in the scenery you develop; and to look at how technical advances can increase reliability and allow for a more complex layout.

You may be creating a layout with a view to exhibiting it. I will show you how you can create an impact, make your layout stand out from the others, and ensure that all the elements blend together. I will help to ensure that your layout runs reliably and is easy to operate at an exhibition.

Moorcock Junction is set in the Yorkshire Dales, with rolling hills and more sheep than people (Andy Calvert). For each layout I give the builder's name, but many layouts will have been sold, as this one, or in a few cases scrapped.

WHAT IS N GAUGE?

'N gauge' or 'N scale' refers to using 9mm-gauge track to represent standard-gauge track. This is accurate for a scale of 1:160, which is used in the USA and on the Continent. For historical reasons British N gauge uses 1:148 scale models running on 9mm track, and in Japan models are 1:150 scale running on 9mm track representing either standard or 3ft 6in gauge. A further complication is British 2mm FineScale, which is 1:152 scale running on 9.42mm-gauge track. All the layouts and models illustrated are to British N gauge unless otherwise stated. You can use models to 1:150 or 1:152 scale alongside 1:148 models, but models to 1:160 scale are sufficiently different that care is needed. Buildings should fit in, as should vehicles if they are not put next to a similar and obviously larger vehicle. However, rolling stock, such as a continental van, is likely to look wrong.

Many aspects of railway modelling are the same whatever scale you choose, but N gauge has some particular benefits. One is that you have a lot more space for scenery. A 2ft (60cm) deep scenic baseboard with a twin-track main line in O gauge only has space for a low-relief building. In OO you can model a row or two of houses or a river. But in N you can fit in a big factory, a housing estate, or a considerable area of countryside.

N gauge has space for long trains. A twelve-coach train in O would be nearly 20ft (6m) long, and most layouts are not that long! Even in OO you are likely to want to shorten the trains. But in N it is less than 6ft (2m). This makes N particularly good for modelling main lines. Even with limited space, you can still run five- or six-coach trains.

In N gauge, the fiddle yard holds a lot more trains. You can fit ten times as much stock in a given area as in O. However, because the fiddle yard is bigger, it will be more complex and difficult to operate, so

Basingstoke models the four-track Southern Region main line, with a double-track Western Region line joining. It runs full length, twelve-coach trains.

Totnes is one of the finest scenic layouts on the exhibition circuit, with a superb backscene blended with the scenery.

for large layouts, the design of the fiddle yard is very important. It is an ideal area for automation, which can make operation simpler and more enjoyable.

You should think about the backscene from the start, since in N gauge it can transform a layout. It should blend as seamlessly as possible with the colours and scenery on the layout.

While N-gauge models are very small and it is difficult to see details unless very close up, digital cameras reveal a lot more, and in a large part your layout will be judged on photographs. I recommend taking photographs regularly when modelling, so you can correct defects that only show up on camera.

NEW TECHNOLOGIES

Digital technologies have made a big impact on railway modelling with DCC (direct command control), but this is only the start. Low cost computers such as the Arduino and Raspberry Pi can connect together points, signals, train detectors and train control to provide automation. Automation can prevent operational errors, deal with repetitive operator tasks, and operate signals that otherwise you might not change.

The main reason for the dramatic improvement in the quality of N-gauge models over the last thirty years is the introduction of new manufacturing

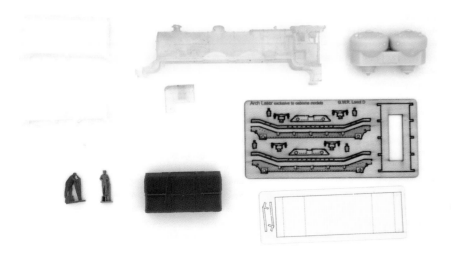

From top left, clockwise: A pair of wagon bodies printed by Shapeways; LMS Patriot body printed by Shapeways; resin-cast Prestwin wagon body (2mm SA); laser-cut kit for GWR Loriot from Osborns Models; 3D-printed BM container from Osborns; 3D-printed figures from ModelU.

technologies. Some have become compact and cheap enough for modellers to own.

3D printing is the technology most talked about: resin 3D printers are available for a few hundred pounds and can produce superb results. Computer printers that print directly on to a model are coming down in price, though are still too expensive for individuals. Laser cutters and CNC milling machines are close to being affordable, but few modellers can justify having them. I have not written about how to use these technologies, partly because they are constantly evolving, but mainly because most modellers will not need to use them. I have bought many 3D-printed, CNC-milled and laser-cut items, but have never designed any myself. Even if you create your own digital designs, you can send them off to be 3D printed, laser cut, or made into decals.

In the future, modelling will increasingly be at a computer rather than the workbench. I use CorelDRAW to create artwork for decals and etched components, and Photoshop for backscenes and sides of buildings. Time spent learning to use drawing and photo-editing software is likely to be well spent.

CHAPTER ONE

TOOLS, ADHESIVES, SOLDER

TOOLS

I have a lot of tools – I like buying them! I've started with the basic tools I use most of the time, then listed some 'nice-to-have' tools that are useful for certain work.

BASIC TOOLS

Pliers: I use a pair of miniature long-nosed pliers all the time, sometimes a similar pair of round-nosed pliers for bending wire into a curve, and occasionally larger pliers to grip something more firmly. A pair of long-nosed pliers with the nose ground very thin is useful for adjusting hand-built track, and parallel-jaw pliers make a good hand vice.

Tweezers: I have a number of different tweezers, all stainless steel (to avoid solder sticking) and with fine points.

Files: An old 6in (15cm) medium file gets a lot of use, particularly on plastic. 12in (30cm) files in various cuts are reserved for filing metal – I look after these carefully and store them in a felt-lined drawer so they don't rub against other tools. I have a variety of needle files: the two I use most are a half-round and a knife-edged file. Smaller needle files are useful for small spaces. Use emery boards (nail files) for filing plastic and card, the sort with a card centre. A 1mm-diameter round file is extremely useful for opening out small holes. They are known as 'seconds files' and are available from suppliers of jewellers' tools.

Knives: Practically the only knife I use is a scalpel. The other knife I have is one with a snap-off blade: it is good for shaping foam when making scenery with a new blade fully extended.

My 'workbench' is a rectangle of MDF with a lip of thin wood fitted round three sides to stop things falling off, and varnished to seal it. On top of this is a self-healing green cutting mat for most cutting, and a rectangle of 'Tufnol' sheet on which to cut out etches and solder. Suitable small blocks are available to buy at many exhibitions or on the internet. On one corner is a watchmaker's vice. Together with a few basic tools, it is easy to move if I want to work elsewhere. It is small, as I often travel by public transport: if I used a car I would have made it bigger. You need plenty of light, a couple of spotlights, and if possible, additional room lighting, such as spotlights pointing at the walls to give indirect light.

Scalpel with a retractable blade. I prefer these to simple handles, as they are much safer for carrying. It is fitted with my preferred #15 blade, a small curved blade, though most modellers I know prefer a larger, straight blade, #11.

Callipers: My favourite tool is a set of 4in (100mm) digital callipers. I do all my measuring with them. For N gauge, this size is better than the more common 6in (150mm). They will measure either imperial or metric, and can be locked to a particular width. They are useful for cutting strips off plastic sheet, as shown in the photos.

When you want to cut a rectangle of plastic to fit inside a wagon, the only tool you need is callipers. Set them to the width of the hole, then lock them in that position with the screw.

Run them down the edge of a sheet of plasticard, putting pressure on the jaw towards the middle of the sheet so it scores a line. Bend the plasticard and it will snap cleanly along the line. Scoring and bending is the recommended way to cut plasticard, better than cutting through with a knife. Repeat to cut to length.

Rulers: I use rulers mainly as straight-edges. Most are steel, though a favourite is a transparent plastic ruler with a metal strip on one edge, that I use when cutting card. It is useful to be able to see what is under the ruler when positioning it, and a grid drawn on the plastic helps you to check it is square to what you are cutting.

Drills: A set of drills ranging from 0.3mm up to 2mm covers nearly everything. The 0.3mm and 0.35mm drills break easily and blunt more quickly than larger drills. As you will probably use these sizes more than any others, buy a packet of ten extra ones. I use 0.35mm rather than 0.30mm when possible as I don't break as many. I do nearly all my drilling with the drill in a pin vice, particularly for small holes: you are likely to break them if you use a mini-drill. Remove small drills from the hole frequently to clear the swarf, as they don't clear themselves as well as larger drills. When drilling

Most modellers have a cheap vice with jaws that are not properly parallel, and can wobble. It is difficult to work on small objects with such a vice. Spend perhaps double on a precision watchmaker's vice, which is much easier to use.

metal either by hand or with an electric drill, use a little standard oil or saliva as a lubricant, as it speeds drilling and helps preserve the drill.

BUYING TOOLS

Quality tools work better and last longer. I buy a lot of my tools from jeweller's tool suppliers such as CousinsUK and Shesto, both online. Their prices are very reasonable and the quality is good.

Clamps: Clamps are useful, for example for holding work while glue sets. It is worth having a variety of shapes and sizes. Small bulldog clips and clothespegs are good when soldering etches.

Soldering iron: Your soldering iron is an important tool, and a good one need not cost a lot if you shop around. Go for a temperature-controlled iron. As well as letting you set the temperature,

My temperature-controlled iron and stand. Buy a brass wool-tip cleaning pot such as the one shown: they work better than the old-fashioned damp sponge, and don't need to be kept moist. Use it regularly when soldering and your tip will stay in good condition. The small pot is 'tip tinner', to use if the tip gets very dirty. Push the hot iron into it, then wipe it in the cleaning pot; repeat until it is clean. Never file the tip to clean it, as it has a thin iron coating that you will remove.

they heat up faster than normal irons. The ones that have a separate station with the controls are easier to use. A chisel bit is suitable for most work, though you might want other bits such as a conical bit. If the iron is not one of the big brands, I recommend buying spare bits with the iron as they may be difficult to find later. You need a stable stand for it, and many come with one. If necessary fix it to a block of wood. When you finish soldering, clean the tip and add a small amount of solder before turning off. This will preserve the tip and extend its life.

Saws: A razor saw is good for making fine cuts in both plastic and metal. One with fine teeth will do most things. For large items a junior hacksaw is better. For cutting out intricate shapes in metal, use a piercing (or jewellers') saw – these are also useful for cutting out holes in plastic sheet. Get one where the length of the frame is adjustable.

Scissors: A sharp pair of scissors is one of the most useful tools you can have, together with a pair of tin snips for cutting sheet metal. Side cutters will cut and strip wires, but you need special cutters for steel wire. Track cutters are (as you might guess) for cutting rails – they cut dead straight on one side. Do not use them on anything harder than rail.

Broach or reamer: A cutting broach or reamer is the easiest and most accurate way of opening out a hole that is too small; it is better than a drill as it stays centred. For N gauge get one of the sets that goes from 0.45mm to 1.4mm (these are the sizes at the widest part; they overlap so there is one suitable for any hole from about 0.25mm to 1.4mm).

Fibreglass brush: A fibreglass brush will remove heavy or hard deposits, such as on a very dirty loco, or excess solder on a metal kit. Be careful, however: the brush is fierce and you can easily remove paint, or even parts of the model if used on plastic. Fragments of glass break off and can get embedded in your hands, causing itching and some pain (in essence itching powder), so use gloves and work so that bits drop to the floor rather than on the bench.

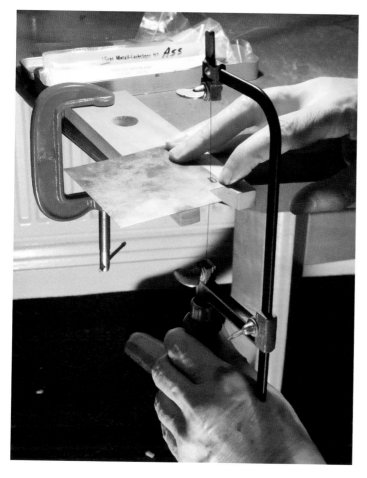

Using a piercing saw. Clamp a 'sawing pin' to the edge of your bench – this is just a rectangle of wood or metal with a narrow V-shaped slot in it; it is easy to make one out of scrap. Select a suitable blade: the gap between the teeth must be no more than about a third the thickness of the sheet being cut. However, do not use one finer than needed, as the thin ones break more often. I suggest having 2/0, 4/0 and 6/0 size blades. Mark clearly the line you want to cut: in the photo the area round the line was blackened with a marker pen before scribing the line. An alternative is to stick a paper drawing on to the metal and cut through it.

To cut a hole in the middle of a sheet, drill a hole large enough to take the blade, inside where you are cutting. Clamp one end of the blade in the handle end – note that, unlike most saws, the teeth must be facing the handle because the saw cuts on the pull stroke, not the push stroke. Put the blade through the hole, then clamp the other end of the blade. Loosen the adjustment on the top of the frame and open it out until the blade is taut (it pings when you flick it); then lock the frame. Lubricate the blade: beeswax is traditional, but vegetable oil or soap will work.

Put the work on the saw table positioned so you will be cutting away from yourself, with the handle of the saw below the work. Lift up the saw, then let it come down pressed against the metal. Hold the saw loosely and do not use much force, as the work is done by the weight of the saw. Move the work around as you cut so you are always cutting away from yourself. Parts of broken blades can be reused by shortening the frame.

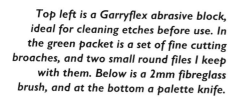

Top left is a Garryflex abrasive block, ideal for cleaning etches before use. In the green packet is a set of fine cutting broaches, and two small round files I keep with them. Below is a 2mm fibreglass brush, and at the bottom a palette knife.

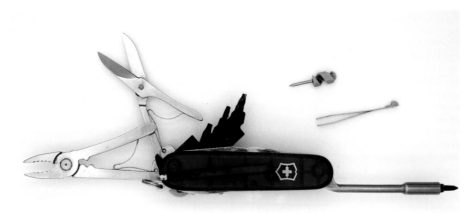

I always carry a 'Cybertool' Swiss army knife. It has (amongst other things) scissors, tweezers, pliers, a miniature screwdriver, and a screwdriver with interchangeable bits. I find I can do most N-gauge loco maintenance with it.

Palette knife: A palette knife is a sort of mini trowel, and is good for applying and smoothing filler, both for scenic work and on models. You can get these at art shops and online.

NICE-TO-HAVE TOOLS

You can do without these tools, but it may take longer or be more difficult to achieve accuracy. You might have access to them at your model railway club.

Cutters: A pair of cutters with hardened steel edges will cut piano wire; places such as Screwfix sell them. Sprue cutters help to get plastic parts off the sprue: I prefer the tweezer-action type to the ones like pliers. Look in the foot-care section of Boots for interesting small cutters.

Drills: A mini-drill makes drilling small holes easier and faster, and is a real boon if you have a lot to do. I only use it for drills of 0.5mm or larger – smaller ones break too easily. You can use it with a cutting disk for hard metal such as piano wire, and for cutting rail – it is about the only way to make a gap in already laid track. You should always wear some eye protection when using a cutting disk, as they can shatter and fly off. A couple of steel burrs are worth having for removing metal or plastic – for example, removing the posts in the centre of Oxford Diecast coach bodies.

There are many makes of drill to choose from, and a wide range of prices. Get one with a good range of speeds. I prefer a chuck to collets as it is faster to use, even if slightly less accurate. One drill to look at is the Proxon Micromot 60/EF; they have a cordless version if you prefer that.

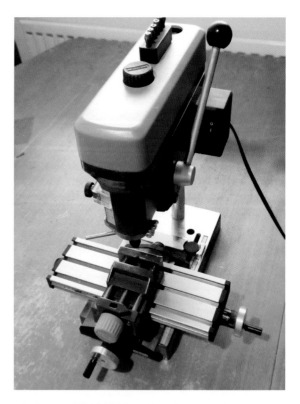

My Proxon TBM 220 bench drill. On the left side is an adjustable depth stop, and on top are the collets for different-sized drills. I have added the KT 70 compound table, which lets you move the work precise distances in any direction.

A bench drill – a vertically mounted drill – makes drilling accurate vertical holes easy, and small drill bits are less likely to break than with a hand-held drill. You can use them for light milling with a milling tool, for example on plastic. A cheaper alternative is a bench stand for your mini-drill.

Styrene cutter: This tool cuts styrene strip to exact lengths. If you do a lot of building from styrene they save time and give greater accuracy. When cutting thick strip, the blade tends to go at an angle, so the cut is not vertical; it is better to make a shallow cut and then bend the strip to complete the cut.

Etch bending tool ('hold and fold'): This tool helps bend etches along straight lines. It is useful if you make a lot of etched metal kits, though a good vice is almost as good. They come in a wide variety of sizes.

Resistance soldering unit: This unit has a transformer that supplies a very large current (typically 40 amps) at a few volts. The earth contact is attached to the metal, solder paste or solder plus flux is put on the joint, then a carbon probe wired to the positive is put against the work where it is to be soldered. The current is turned on briefly by a foot switch. The resistance at the tip of the probe

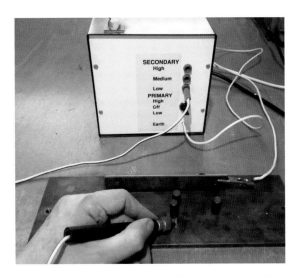

Resistance soldering unit. Six different power levels can be selected: for most work in N gauge a low one is all you need; the higher ones can vaporize small etches. The high settings let you solder to large pieces of metal. The return lead is attached to the steel plate by a crocodile clip; the work is held against the plate by magnets and the tip of the probe.

causes the area round it to get very hot and melt the solder; you can move the probe along a seam to solder all the way along. The probe can help hold the work in place. Joints can be made with a minimum of solder, and are excellent for joining two sheets of metal. Some use them occasionally, others use them all the time for non-electrical soldering. If you are interested there is often someone demonstrating one at the larger exhibitions.

Bench power supply: This is a variable voltage DC supply, with an adjustable current limiter; 0–15 volts is a good range. It shows the voltage and current taken. Cheap ones can cost less than a DC train controller, and are very useful if you do a lot of fiddling with electrics or electronics, or just for testing locos.

Multi-cutter tool: This has an oscillating head that can be fitted with a variety of tools. The saw blades will rapidly cut a rectangular hole in a baseboard, or trim a sheet of ply on the end of a board to the height you want for the scenery.

This styrene cutter has a cast-metal base and metal arm; cheaper ones are plastic and can flex when cutting.

My old bench power supply: modern ones have a digital readout. The current limiter reduces the chances of accidental damage. It also supplies fixed voltage DC at 5V and 12V.

A multi-cutter tool; cordless is more convenient than mains-powered. It is shown with the small saw blade, suitable for making holes in baseboards. The larger saw blade is good for trimming ply, the tool on the right is a sander, and the other a scraper.

ADHESIVES

Whatever the glue, grease or oil on the surfaces will reduce the strength of the bond. Wash plastic, metal or resin first with diluted isopropyl alcohol, then wipe dry with a paper towel.

A few of the adhesives I use regularly. I use Roket Card Glue and a gel superglue the most.

PVA GLUE

This is the best glue for paper and card, and will bond many other materials, though the bond is not particularly strong on non-porous materials. I use it for fixing things to the baseboard. I like Roket Card Glue for making buildings as it has a very good grab; it is fine for other work, too.

PLASTIC GLUES

More accurately plastic glues are solvents, and they work by dissolving a little of the surface of the plastic on both sides of the joint. This mixes, then sets as the solvent evaporates, forming a weld, so a good joint is as strong as the plastic. They only work on bare plastic: if it is painted use something else. I use Butanone for most plastic kits and for styrene strip, as it grips well while still allowing a bit of time for adjustment. Many model shops sell it, or it can be bought in larger quantities online. Apply it with an old paintbrush, as it tends to ruin brushes. Run the wetted brush along the side of the joint, with the parts held together, and the solvent is sucked into the joint by capillary action. For a really strong joint, rub the two parts together after applying the adhesive so any irregularities are flattened or filled in.

Sometimes for larger items when I want more time, I use Revell Professional, which is thicker and applied to one side of the joint before assembling. These two glues will glue styrene, and Butanone works on many, but not all other plastics. If Butanone doesn't work I try Plastic-Weld, which bonds very quickly. Do not leave the cap off or loose, as it evaporates quickly.

Note there are some plastics, such as polythene, that cannot be glued, and others where an epoxy or cyanoacrylate glue is needed. Butanone will bond plastic to some porous materials such as wood strip: it seems that some of the dissolved plastic penetrates the wood, then when it dries, it forms a mechanical bond. I have managed to glue styrene to some 'impossible' plastics by first scoring the surface of the hard plastic with a knife held at a shallow angle to lift small flaps and give the styrene something to lock on to.

EPOXY RESIN GLUES

These give a strong bond on most materials. You mix the two parts, then you have a limited time in which to use them. Before gluing, clean any grease off, then slightly abrade the surface with fine wet-and-dry to help the glue key. Wash to get the dust off, and allow to dry completely. Do this and you will get a very strong bond. Normal epoxy is workable for about one hour, and sets fully hard in twenty-four. You can get a 'rapid' version, which sets faster but is only workable for five minutes, but I don't use this as it is not as strong. If you want the joint to set faster, just put it in an oven set to 50°C for an hour or so. I found the rapid version became unusable after a couple of years, while I am still using some ten-year-old standard adhesive.

SUPERGLUES (CYANOACRYLATE GLUES)

These glues will stick most things, including skin and metals, though they are not good on ABS plastic, polythene or leather. The two basic varieties are liquid and gel, and there are some special types such as odourless (which does not fog glazing), and ones developed for gluing plastics. The liquid version comes in different thicknesses: the thinner it is, the faster it bonds – the very thin (hot) versions are almost instantaneous. You can apply thick and gel glues to one surface, but for the thin versions it is better to apply it to the edge of the joint and let it get sucked in. The strongest joints are when there is only a very thin layer of glue.

The gel versions are semi-solid and I find them easier to work with, as they stay put and give you a few seconds to make adjustments. They are slightly flexible compared to the liquid glues, though they do not form as strong a bond (but it is still very good).

For either type, do not apply the glue directly from the bottle to your work: put a little on a scrap bit of plastic or shiny card, and transfer it to your work on the tip of a pin. Buy small tubes of gel glue, as they only last a few months once opened. Have a bottle of medium liquid glue as well.

Superglue is quite brittle, and can break off if knocked. It is best for parts that are held together mechanically, for example by a tab in a slot, and relatively poor for attaching detail to a flat surface: in this case solder or epoxy will be better. Always clean the nozzle after use, and don't leave glue in the nozzle, where it will set solid. Keep the glues cool and dry to extend their life.

OTHER FIXATIVES

Contact adhesives such a UHU and Bostik are sometimes useful, but can be messy. I occasionally use them when I know I might want to take things apart later, as you can usually prise joints apart. For larger areas spraycans are good, as they ensure a thin, even coat of adhesive.

Copydex: A latex rubber adhesive sold for fixing carpets. It is excellent for any sort of fabric, and will bond most materials. It is very resistant to bangs and shocks. It is good for sticking cork to a baseboard.

A number of the less permanent adhesives, although double-sided tape and Pritt can be used for permanent joints. On the right are the two fillers I use.

Insta Stik: A strong, general-purpose polyure-thane foam adhesive, sold at DIY and tool outlets, and applied using a sealant gun. I use it for sticking foam and wood when making scenery; you need to clamp it for five minutes while it foams. It dries hard in under an hour, and will fill substantial gaps. It is advisable to wear gloves, as it sticks extremely well to skin and it takes days to get it all off. When you finish using it, let some glue come out of the gun and form a knob over the end of the spout. This will keep the remainder usable for several months. It can be useful for jobs around the house as well.

Double-sided tape: This tape is easy to use without making any mess, and can give a strong bond. There are two main types. One is very thin and is best for joining two completely flat surfaces, or when at least one material is flexible and can be pressed on. It can be used for fixing track down, or a small rectangle can be used to hold a weight or load in place on a wagon. It is fairly easy to prise apart later if you need to, especially if it is warmed with a hair dryer. The other type has a flexible layer about 1mm thick, so can be used on surfaces that are not flat. It is very sticky: I use small squares for holding wires and electronic components in place. You can unstick items and put them back many times.

Blu Tack and Tacky Wax: These are tempo-rary fixatives. I use them for emergency repairs at exhibitions, such as to hold a coupling rigid when a wagon keeps uncoupling.

Milliput: An epoxy putty, which can also act as an adhesive. I use the Superfine White. There are two components that have to be kneaded together for five minutes before use. It can be given a very smooth finish by going over it with a damp palette knife, and it dries rock hard. Its down side is the time it takes to mix it, so I often use a ready-mixed filler such as Squadron, though it is not as strong.

SOLDER AND FLUX

You will be familiar with cored electrical solder, which contains rosin flux. It is ideal for electrical soldering, but not so good for models as it tends to form blobs on a surface, rather than flow on to it. The rosin flux forms a protective layer; it can be painted over, but is better removed. Rosin is less active than most other fluxes, which is why it need not be cleaned off, but it means it is more difficult to get a good joint. Stronger fluxes will cope with some dirt or oxide on the metal to be soldered. For metal kits I use either a separate flux plus a solder suited to what I am doing, or solder paste: a mix of finely ground solder and flux, which you put on the joint.

My preferred fluxes are dilute phosphoric acid (widely available), or Powerflow plumber's flux. The latter will work on 'difficult' metals such as steel.

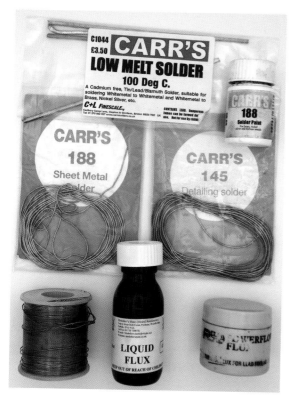

The solders and fluxes that I use regularly.

Apply flux to the joint, and put the solder on the tip of the iron, or put a small slice on the flux. An alternative is to use 'solder balls' on the work: small balls of solder sold in various sizes. Either way you don't need to hold the solder. The disadvantage of a flux other than rosin is that you *must* wash off any remains before painting. If left on, over time it reacts with the metal and causes paint to bubble or loosen.

For etched metal kits, I mostly use Carr's 188°C sheet solder. It will go into thin layers, and can make joints with minimal solder. For adding details I sometimes use Carr's 145°C detailing solder with a lower melting point, so you can use a cooler iron, which prevents previously soldered joints coming apart. If a fillet of solder is needed to reinforce the inside of a joint I may use electrical solder. For small parts I often use solder paste, and almost always when using my resistance soldering unit. Low-melt solder is needed for white-metal kits: I prefer the 100°C version to the 70°C as it is stronger.

I do most of my work with the iron set to a temperature of 325°C as I use lead solders. The iron must be hot enough to melt the solder quickly, but if it is hotter than needed it reduces the life of the tip, and risks damaging the work. An iron that is not temperature controlled needs to be a little hotter to start with, because when you start soldering it is less able to maintain the temperature. When working on large pieces of metal the iron may need to be hotter than usual to provide extra heat; otherwise use a larger iron or a resistance soldering unit. With lower-melt solders I reduce the temperature, perhaps to 200°C.

Lead solders are easier to use than modern lead-free solders. Lead-free solders are now used commercially because of the health hazards of prolonged exposure to lead, but for occasional hobby use just be careful to wash your hands afterwards. With lead-free solder the iron needs to be a little hotter, as these solders have a higher melting point.

CHAPTER TWO

MAKING IT LOOK REAL

How do you make your layout look like a model of a real railway, rather than a train set?

Start by choosing an area of the country to model, and make everything match that area. Create railway buildings of the architecture of the company modelled, and ensure that other buildings are built from materials that would be used in that area. The landscape needs to be an accurate representation, be it flat fenland or steep valleys, with crops, trees, fences and walls that are correct for the area.

Equally importantly, choose a narrow time period. A photograph can often be dated to within ten years, not just by the trains and vehicles, but by the style of people's clothing, the advertisements, road markings, construction materials, and the types of television aerials or satellite dishes. It all gives consistency, so when people view your layout they are transported to a particular part of the country at a particular time. Features that are out of place spoil that illusion.

The simplest way to achieve this is to make a model of a real place. When you do this it is surprising how many features you model that you would not have thought of including. If an exact model of a location is impractical, you can still get a good representation through compromises such as shortening the platforms and train lengths by a third, or reducing five sidings to three, or increasing the curvature of the line. Researching a location takes time, but it is a very enjoyable part of railway modelling.

If a single location doesn't suit, consider merging the features of several nearby locations. For example, use the track plan from one location, but add the dairy that is at the larger station a few miles away, and put the interesting pub that is a mile down the track on the edge of the layout.

You will have to make a lot of the buildings yourself, but that will make your layout stand out from half-a-dozen other layouts that have an identical row of high-street shops. You can still use commer-

Wickwar is an accurate model of a small country station on a busy secondary main line. I have worked on this layout at Farnham & District MRC over the last ten years, and examples from it appear throughout the book.

Stoney Lane Depot is not a real location, but combines real buildings and features of the area around Stewarts Lane Depot to create a scene that is instantly recognizable as South London in the 1980s/1990s.

cially available buildings if they happen to suit, but don't use them straight out of the box. Walk down a street of houses built fifty years ago and no two will be the same. They will differ not just in minor details, such as the colour of the paint: windows will have been changed, gardens converted for car parking, garage and loft conversions, conservatories added.

Don't feel it is necessary to fill the baseboards. Empty spaces help make it look more real – most country goods yards had lots of space around the sidings. It is only in towns and cities that space was tight, and even then there will be waste ground. Your station doesn't need to have every rail-served industry imaginable. Settle for one or two, and you can still justify having a wide range of traffic for industries further along the line or accessed by road.

Railway companies had their own styles, and not just of buildings: the type of fencing, and the layout of the track and the station all varied. The Midland went to huge lengths to avoid facing points, and even in BR days you could see this.

Even if you choose not to model a specific location, base your track plan on a real location, cut down and compressed if necessary. The track layout will look authentic, because it is.

Tracks running parallel to the board edges can look artificial, particularly at the front. Models with the track angled or on a slight curve look much better.

Railway lines are very rarely level with the surrounding ground. They were built so they were at the average height of the ground they passed through, so they spend as much time on embankments as in cuttings. Next time you are on a train, notice how often the line goes from a cutting to an embankment and back again – often within less than half a mile. Unfortunately many models have track on a flat baseboard and the scenery is built up from there, which can look artificial. Embankments are not only realistic, but trains going over embankments look better than ones in the bottom of a cutting. Roads are rarely level or at the same height as the railway line.

Rather than a flat-topped baseboard, choose what is known as an open frame baseboard, which is just a frame with bracing. Glue foam blocks into the frame and shape them how you want, adding a ply top where needed for track. It is then easy to have roads and streams that are lower than the tracks.

Modern close-coupling mechanisms allow close-coupled trains to go round tight curves, but when viewed from the outside of the curve, large gaps can

The sweeping curve on Law Junction greatly adds to the appeal of this layout.

be seen between the ends of coaches. So avoid tight curves on the scenic parts of the layout. A three-foot (1m) radius curve is massive by N standards, but on the real railway would probably be considered too tight for passenger trains. The latest high-speed lines have a minimum radius of 7 kilometres (4 miles): with scale curves in N a basic oval needs an area larger than most football pitches!

Use the longest turnouts you can – ideally nothing shorter than a Peco long on the main running lines, and nothing shorter than medium in sidings. These are just about acceptable for 1950s track, but are short for more modern main-line track.

Keep the colours and finish consistent and harmonious. Make the colours used for grass consistent with the layout, and match them to the backscene. Avoid having some items glossy and similar items very matt. This applies not only to rolling stock, but to vehicles and even buildings. Aim for a consistent level of weathering.

MAKING A LAYOUT DIFFERENT

Many people model a GWR or BR(W) terminus on a summer's day. It is in many ways an ideal choice for a small layout, with a wide range of stock available.

But your layout will not stand out, and it will be in direct comparison with other very fine models. So you might want to consider doing something a little different.

One way is to include some spectacular scenery: the deep gorge on Chee Tor is an example. Or it might be a man-made feature such as a large bridge or viaduct. Rivers always look impressive when modelled; they usually come with an interesting bridge, and need not take up a lot of space.

You could model a large, rail-connected industry – not just a single factory building, but at least a portion of a large site. N gauge has the space for it – for example a chemical works, or a coal mine, or an iron works. It will need a lot of research, but you will be able to impress viewers by explaining what all the different buildings were for.

Trying to find a railway company that has not been modelled is difficult, and there will be little or no stock available off the shelf. However, you can avoid the periods most commonly modelled, for example the mid-sixties. If you model pre-grouping, you will have to make most of the stock from kits, or scratch-build it. Scratch-building is easier in 2mm fine scale because the 2mm Scale Association sells a wide range of components, such as driving wheels

Chee Tor (2mm FS) has amazing scenery, with the railway just a small detail. (Manchester MRC.)

and gears. The grouping period is much better served in N. You will have to build some stock, but there are kits available.

For later periods almost all the stock you need should be available in 'ready-to-run' (RTR). The early days of BR, around 1949, are rarely modelled, and have an interesting mix of grouping liveries, wartime liveries and early BR standard liveries. Privatization introduced many new liveries, and they changed regularly.

Castle Hill (Finescale N, 1:148 scale with 9.5mm track) has a spectacular GWR lattice bridge.

Well-modelled water such as this on Loch Tat sticks in the memory.

Most layouts are set on a sunny summer's day – I've seen only a few layouts set in winter. Those with a light covering of snow seem to look best: thick snowfalls can look like cotton wool and hide detail. Autumn can look spectacular, but again is rarely modelled.

While modelling a thunderstorm would be difficult (the thunder and lightning is easy, but the rain might upset locos!), it would be possible to model shortly after heavy rain. I don't remember seeing this done, but there is plenty to model: puddles, damp roads with dry lines where tyres have been, muddy paths, gushing streams.

Instead of putting track along the front of the layout more or less parallel to the edge, more

Witney Euston (2mm FS) is a very convincing model of a winter scene – it makes you feel cold looking at it!

Queen's Street Goods (2mm FS) shows a northern goods yard but from an unusual end view through the railings beyond the buffer stops.

scenery might be put in front of the railway, or lines could come in from the side and then curve away from the viewer to a junction going backwards. Some layouts have the track deep in a cutting, others have it on an embankment or viaduct viewed from below the level of the track.

Wenford Bridge (2mm FS) is a small GWR station with a moving tractor and trailer, and a crane that loads and unloads the trailer. It always attracts a crowd at exhibitions.

Any sort of animation draws attention. Moving vehicles are discussed later. Other options are loading and unloading wagons, and industrial machinery.

Sound effects can be included, for example loco sounds using DCC. Don't overdo them: some of the most unpopular layouts to be next to at exhibitions are those with constant loud noise. At one exhibition a very effective use of sound was a seaside layout, with the faint noise of breaking waves and a few gulls. It was so quiet you hardly noticed it, but it added atmosphere.

With a long layout, it is a good idea to have one or two large buildings on the front to break it up into separate scenes; it is even better if the large buildings are interesting and a focal point in themselves.

CHAPTER THREE

BASEBOARDS

Even for a permanent layout it makes sense to build it on boards that can be separated should you move house or want to sell it – though track and wiring might be continuous across the joints. But for layouts that have to be taken down when not in use, or taken to exhibitions, it has to be on multiple boards that can be rapidly assembled.

Don't underestimate how important ease of assembly is: time spent putting it up and taking it down is modelling time you are losing. Our previous club layout took over an hour of hard work by four or five people to erect and the same time again to take down, and as a result it was rarely put up completely. Our new layout can be erected by two people in less than half an hour, and it is put up most

weeks. It is admittedly a much smaller layout, but equally importantly the baseboards weigh a fraction of those on the previous layout so are easier and less tiring to handle.

SIZE

The boards must be small enough that they are easy to handle. Do they need to be small enough that the layout can be erected by one person?

A 3ft by 4ft (1m by 1.2m) board will fit in a hatchback, and most will take a board up to 5ft (1.5m). But even a lightweight baseboard of that size is awkward for one person to handle. It is often useful to be able to transport a single board in a hatchback

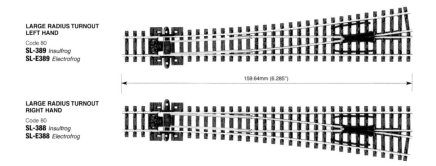

PECO STREAMLINE CODE 80
TURNOUTS AND CROSSINGS PLANS

LARGE RADIUS TURNOUT
LEFT HAND

Code 80
SL-389 *Insulfrog*
SL-E389 *Electrofrog*

159.64mm (6.285")

LARGE RADIUS TURNOUT
RIGHT HAND

Code 80
SL-388 *Insulfrog*
SL-E388 *Electrofrog*

One of the Peco templates that can be downloaded and printed from www. peco-uk. com. (Reproduced with the permission of Pritchard Patent Product Co Ltd.)

These plans are produced by the manufacturers and may be
reproduced by modellers for the purpose of layout building.
Commercial copying or reproduction prohibited.
© PRITCHARD PATENT PRODUCT CO. LTD, BEER, DEVON EX12 3NA ENGLAND

Use this scale bar to check that your printer is printing at 100%

0 inches   1   2   3   4   5   6   7   8   9   10

0 cm 1 2 3 4 5 6 7 8 9 10 11 12 13 14 15 16 17 18 19 20 21 22 23 24 25

even if you normally use a van, and boards must be small enough to get them through doorways and up and down stairs. Think about what you will use to transport the boards before settling on a particular board size.

You need to be able to reach all the track. Two feet (60cm) is as far as you can lean over comfortably to get at stock, while three feet (1m) is the maximum.

Keep the boards as low as is practical; a removable backscene helps a lot, as it means the boards need only be as high as the highest scenery.

Don't build the baseboards until you have decided exactly what will be going on them – time spent planning will avoid mistakes that are difficult to correct, such as a board joint directly under a point, or a curve that is too tight. I like to draw out the design full size on the back of old rolls of wall-

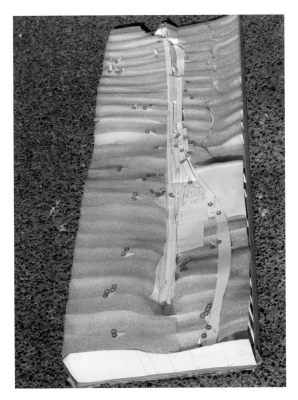

We made a very basic 3D model from card and foam of the area around Wickwar station when we started planning Wickwar. The red dots show the places from which we took photographs.

paper. If using Peco points, print templates, then cut them out and stick them in position. Or you can use a software package, but make sure it has support for the type of track you intend using, such as Peco code 55. The Templot drawing software is excellent if you are hand-building track, but if using commercial track then a simpler package is more appropriate.

Making a rough, small-scale model will give a better idea of how the final layout will look, and how viewing angles work.

The boards are usually all made the same size and shape, but they needn't be. Think what baseboard shapes and sizes will be best. The most important factor is that you can't have points across baseboard joints, and it is preferable to have junctions well away from joints for best running. The front of the layout doesn't have to be straight – if it curves slightly inwards this has the advantage at exhibitions of allowing a little more space for spectators.

A board with the station and goods yard needs more depth than one with just plain track.

HIDING JOINTS

A dead-straight trench across a field or road looks odd, and while you can't eliminate joints between boards, a lot can be done to disguise them. If a linear feature such as a wall, hedge or kerb can be made to run next to the joint it will help hide it. Or it could be the edge of a building: the line of the building will distract the eye from the gap. Something to consider is adjusting the size and shape of baseboards so the joints follow features. This might involve having the join between two boards at something other than a right angle to the front.

It is possible to position a building across the joint and make it removable, or to have trees by the joint that can be taken off when packing up the layout. A lift-out area on a thin ply base with a house and garden moves the joint to the edge of the lift-out section, where it can be disguised by a hedge.

After erecting the boards, scatter some loose flock over the join to help hide it – have a small bag of suitable flock to take to exhibitions.

Where a road crosses a join, a sliver of foam of the correct colour glued to the edge of the board will hide any small gap. Make the foam thicker at the top where it is visible so it isn't too much to compress when joining the boards.

JOINING BOARDS

The boards need to be joined securely and accurately; as you will be doing this frequently, it has to be quick and easy. However, an error of a fraction of a millimetre in alignment can result in trains derailing or uncoupling, so you need the boards to locate precisely and with minimal slop.

The ends of the boards need to be solid and unlikely to warp; 9mm or thicker ply is a good choice, or 6mm double thickness where alignment dowels are fitted.

The most accurate method of ensuring alignment is to use pattern-maker's dowels. These are recessed into the ends of the boards, and one of each pair has a brass protrusion that fits into the one on the other board. However, it needs good woodworking skills to fit them accurately. Bullet dowels are easier to fit but not as precise: with these a hole is drilled through both boards while they are clamped together, then the dowels are hammered in. DCC Concepts sells dowels that combine the two: they are hammered into a hole but have the wide lip for greater precision.

Even with these seemingly very precise locators there is some play, so check the tracks are precisely aligned and level before tightening up the boards;

On the left at the top are pattern-maker's dowels, and below bullet dowels, both from Station Road Baseboards. On the right are DCC Concepts dowels fitted to baseboards.

Wickwar uses home-made connectors welded from steel. The foam and ply baseboard edge has been drilled out, and a plug of wood glued in where the connector goes, to increase strength in this critical area.

any adjustment should be made by pushing and pulling on the boards.

The boards must be held together tightly. The simplest method is to use bolts and wing nuts, with

Toggle latches mounted on the sides of the boards are much faster. I recommend buying slightly more expensive ones, which are sprung. The main downside to latches is that they can catch during transport and get damaged. As they hold the outside of the boards these need to be very rigid so they stay tightly together in the centre.

washers glued in place to protect the wood. At least two bolts are needed, one each side of the tracks. The downside of bolts is that they take some time to put in and screw up, and it can be awkward getting underneath to put them in. Have spares as some always go missing.

All the alignment dowels and fasteners must be fitted before you start to lay track.

BASEBOARD CONSTRUCTION

The traditional way to make baseboards was to use a frame of 2 × 4in (5 × 10cm) timber with thick ply on top, and perhaps Sundeala board on top of that. These were certainly robust, but they often needed two fit people to handle them. A beam made of a layer of structural foam with lightweight ply on each side is stronger than timber, less flexible, less affected by heat and damp, and a lot lighter.

Any wood should be painted to seal it against damp – diluted varnish is good. Paint the undersides with white emulsion – it helps show up any wiring, is easy to write on, and when you have to crawl underneath it reflects more light, improving visibility.

For N gauge I strongly recommend open-frame baseboards. Instead of a flat top to the baseboard it is just a frame with a few cross-braces. Blocks of foam are glued into the frame and sculpted to what-

Wickwar baseboards are constructed from 1cm (0.4in) or 2.5cm (1in) thick Styrofoam laminated with 3mm lightweight Gaboon marine ply, glued on with an epoxy adhesive. Large sheets were laminated, then cut into beams. The beams are very light and extremely rigid.

Wickwar open-frame baseboards at an early stage of construction. The right side where the fiddle yard goes is flat, as on a conventional baseboard, and this extends into the scenic area where the track will go. The remainder of the scenic part comprises just blocks of foam, which will be built up as shown in the chapter on scenery. The far end of the central board has ply edging, cut roughly to the shape the scenery will be.

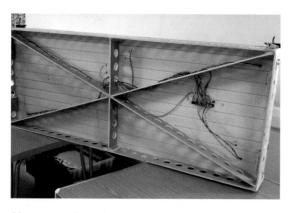

More recently we have made boards with thinner main beams and ply strips for the diagonal bracing. Lighter still is our test-track baseboard, a block of Styrofoam with ply glued round the edges and ply strips underneath to brace it.

ever height is required for scenery, adding strips of ply as needed for railways and roads: it is child's play to have areas both above and below the height of the track. Another advantage of this approach is that the baseboards are lighter.

If you don't feel competent to build your own boards, a number of companies produce laser-cut baseboards, either in standard sizes or to your specification. These usually come as kits for the home builder.

ELECTRICAL CONNECTIONS

As the boards have to be taken apart, electrical connections between them have to be cables with plugs and sockets. The commonest method is a cable and plug on one board, with a clip to secure it during transport, and the matching socket on the next. The controllers and control panels then plug into one of the centre boards.

Getting underneath can be awkward, so mount the sockets on the outside of the rear of the boards where they are easily accessible. Better still, rather than having a cable with a plug on one board, put sockets on both boards and use separate cables with a plug on each end to connect them. You can buy pre-wired cables that are very robust, and are less likely to have failures than ones that are soldered. A dangling cable and plug can get damaged during transport; this is unlikely with a separate cable, and you can have a spare. DB15 (15 pin) or DB25 (25 pin) serial connectors are a good choice; the sockets and cables are widely available.

Rather than connecting cables between boards, I prefer to have cables going from each board to a central electronics box, into which the control panels and controllers also plug. It sounds like more cabling, but it isn't: in fact it often results in less. You can erect any single board and power it up in the club room. Also most of the electronics can be mounted in the central box where they are more accessible if anything goes wrong. There is a single cable to each board rather than the outside boards being at the end of a chain, which reduces resistance and the number of connectors to check when there is a failure.

The sockets on Wickwar are recessed into the rear of each board. The collection above looks more complex than it is, as some sockets are no longer used. The blue Centronics socket is used for track connections, including train-on-track detection sections. The black SCART socket connects two cameras, a monitor, and a separate CBUS used for the roadway. All the other sockets are redundant, replaced by the SCART connector, except the sound socket used for the train whistles. A separate socket (not on this panel) provides servo power and the CBUS for point and signal operation.

Quite often there will be two cables to each board, one with a lot of low-current wires and the other with a few thicker wires for power.

DCC is sometimes sold as only needing two wires, but in practice you end up with rather more for a whole variety of reasons. The main saving comes from using a digital bus to connect points and so on, rather than individual wires, though this can be done for DC as well.

LAYOUT SUPPORTS

The layout must be supported at whatever height is chosen. It is tempting to put the boards on tables, with very short legs that lift the boards to the desired height above the table. The downside of this is that if attending an exhibition you will need a set of tables of the correct size and all the same height. Unfortunately exhibitions have different table sizes available, and some find it difficult to get a matched set of the same height; furthermore tables may be in

short supply, or may have to be hired by the exhibition. So I would avoid this if possible.

LAYOUT HEIGHT

How high should the layout be? For a home layout, a good height is just below eye level when sitting down. Layouts look at their best viewed from eye level because it is the view you have of the real railway. However, if you are going to exhibit the layout there is no right answer and you have to compromise. This is covered later under exhibition layouts.

Legs can be built into the boards – this is usually one pair of legs on each board, and one board with two pairs that needs to be put up first. You cannot forget to take them to an exhibition, but it does add to the weight of the boards, and it means that if you only want to put up part of the layout it has to include the board with four legs. A variant is to make the legs removable, fitting into sockets on the boards.

The other popular system, which I prefer, is to support the boards on a number of separate wooden frames, one per board plus one extra. The frames can be made out of wood, or saw-horse frames can be bought from a DIY shop, though that does fix the height quite low. You can put up single boards, and when working on individual boards the legs will not be in the way.

Some floors are very uneven, and old agricultural halls that were designed to be hosed down have a marked slope. The legs need to be adjustable to get the layout level, so use feet that can be screwed up and down. Even then it is good to have a stock of small wooden blocks for exhibition halls with big height differences.

You can check that boards are in line with each other by sighting along the edges, though that does not guarantee they are level. In N, a small slope can create enough of a gradient that a loco that happily pulled a ten-coach train now struggles with it. We

The frames used on Wickwar. The two parts are hinged together and a chain at the bottom limits how far they open. There is an adjustable foot on each corner. There will be slight differences between frames, so label them so that you always use each one in the same place and orientation. Mark exactly where the frame is to go under each board. The frames at the end of the layout need to be inset from the ends of the boards to prevent them being kicked by operators walking round the ends.

mount spirit levels in a hole on the rear of each board to help get them level; they were taken out of a level from Poundland. Also make sure that the boards are level from front to back.

It is best not to fully tighten the joins between boards until they are level, because when they are not level they may twist and be out of alignment.

BASEBOARD LIDS

A lid over the track and scenery will protect it during transport and storage, and keep dust off. I would always have a lid for an exhibition layout: sooner or later you will have to carry it through rain into the hall.

A lightweight lid can be made from thin ply sides and a block of insulation foam for the top. Alternatively ply can be used throughout, with square timber glued inside the joints to reinforce them.

The lids can be secured by catches, or by a couple of bolts on each side, or Velcro. The inside of a lid is a good place to store and transport flat objects such as display boards.

Sometimes it is possible to avoid having to use a lid by putting a pair of boards together for transport, with one upside down on top of the other, and a light frame holding them in position.

A lid made of insulation foam for the top and sides; hand holds are cut into the ply ends. Heavyweight fabric-reinforced tape bound over the corners protects them from damage. One of the display boards that goes on the end of the layout is bolted inside for transport.

When putting the lids on there is a risk that scenery on the edge of the board may be damaged, so to protect it, ply end boards are placed over the ends before the lids are put on; these are located by a glued-in screw, which acts as a pin.

CHAPTER FOUR

FIDDLE YARDS AND AUTOMATION

When trains go off scene they are usually stored in sidings in the non-scenic area of the layout. These sidings are called fiddle yards. On a large layout they can be complex and boring to operate, so are prime candidates for automation. Any repetitive action on a layout that can be automated makes operation more enjoyable and more reliable.

Automation is useful for signals. It is easy to make signals work, but operators often don't bother changing them.

FIDDLE YARDS

A well designed fiddle yard can make operating a pleasure, but a poor one makes it a task to be dreaded. So if you intend doing a lot of operating, and in particular for a layout you are going to exhibit, think hard about fiddle-yard design. Because N gauge stores a lot more trains in a given area than larger scales, it can have particularly complex fiddle yards.

There are two main configurations of yard: single-ended fiddle yards where trains enter and depart at one end, and double-ended yards where trains enter at one end and depart at the other. Because many N layouts are ovals, the double-ended yard is most common.

Single-ended yards are used on layouts modelling a terminus; double-ended yards are used on continuous run layouts depicting a through line where the two ends are joined round the back. Such a layout might have a single-ended yard as well for branch-line trains. Larger scales often have a single-ended yard at each end of a through station, but in N there is usually space to have a complete oval, which is easier to operate.

Ideally the fiddle yard should be capable of holding all the trains you are likely to run in an operating session, which can mean it has more track and takes more space than the scenic part of the layout. Make

A small, single-track double-ended fiddle yard on Mike le Marie's layout, Kinlocklaggen.

it bigger than you think you will need, because by the time you finish building the layout you will have acquired a lot more trains!

Don't put the tracks too close together. You often need to take trains on and off, and if there are trains on the adjacent roads you can easily knock one of them off the track. Wickwar has tracks at the standard 1.5in (4cm) spacing between centres, and we often wish we had made it 2in (5cm).

On most layouts, particularly those running long trains, there will be a mix of long and short trains. You can cater for this by having the roads of different lengths, or by some roads holding two or more trains.

A large fiddle yard on Northallerton, built by Cleveland Model Railway Club. It depicts two two-track lines joining to form a four-track line. The two closer yards are the up and down yards for one branch. At the far end they duck under the lines of the other branch to avoid crossing on the level.

SINGLE-ENDED YARDS

Most single-ended yards consist of a simple fan of sidings. When connected to a two-track line it is best if the two lines join together before fanning out, so trains can go between any fiddle-yard road and either main line.

With loco-hauled trains the loco needs to be moved to the other end of the train before it returns; with a goods train the brake van needs moving to the back. There may be trains that are always mar-shalled in a particular order – for example, goods

Instead of a lot of points a traverser can be built, a board with multiple parallel tracks that slides so any one of them can be lined up with the layout. It saves on length but needs more width. A variation is a sector plate, where instead of moving sideways the board is pivoted at the far end.

wagons or milk tanks would always be behind pas-senger coaches, so these might need rearranging. It can be tricky re-railing the stock and checking they are coupled up, so often other forms of fiddle yard are used that avoid this need.

Some layouts use a 'turntable': this is a rectangle of baseboard with multiple tracks long enough for the longest train, pivoted in the middle so it can be rotated to line up any track on the turntable with the line (or lines) on the scenic section. When all trains have been sent out and come back they will all be the wrong way round; the whole can then be rotated through 180 degrees, so all the trains are facing the right way again.

Cassettes are popular, particularly for small branch-line layouts. They are train-length, U-shaped

Cassettes used as the fiddle yard on Llangerisech, a 2mm FS layout depicting a substantial terminus at the end of a single-track branch. As well as the main cassette, a separate short cassette is used for locos, joined on to the cassette containing the rest of the train.

boards with a single track running along them. On the end of the layout you put a shelf at a height so a cassette placed on it has its track the same height as the layout. Place the cassette so the track lines up. A socket of some sort holds it in position and provides an electrical connection so a train can run on to it. It is then replaced by another cassette with a different train. The cassette can be turned round before it is replaced to reverse the train, and cassettes of different lengths can be used. The big danger with cassettes is dropping them, or the stock coming out while handling them; there should be a way of blocking the ends to prevent trains rolling off.

While standard track could be laid on the cassette, more commonly the 'track' is just two strips of metal, such as aluminium angle, 9mm apart, screwed or glued to a ply base. This is both cheap and robust.

Goods of particular types are likely to flow in one direction only. For example, full coal wagons may be delivered and empty ones leave, so ideally you need to add and remove such loads in the fiddle yard and on the scenic area.

DOUBLE-ENDED YARDS

These are used on oval layouts where trains run round and round. The most common arrangement

is a set of parallel roads with points at the entry and exit. There are usually separate sets of storage roads in each direction, and a four-track main line usually has four sets.

A space-saving alternative is a vertical stack of tracks of trains that can be moved up and down so one track is level with the layout. It uses very little horizontal space so a lot of trains can be stored, and it is possible to have separate stacks for each running track that can move independently. However, building one yourself and getting it working reliably is a considerable engineering challenge. A company called Nelevator made them, but I can't remember ever seeing one in use on an exhibition layout.

For oval layouts there are two configurations of baseboard that might be used. The most compact is known as a dumbbell. At each end is a section that is not scenic, where the tracks turn through 180 degrees and return on the rear of the baseboards. The other boards might be split two-thirds scenic/ one-third fiddle yard.

The alternative is a complete oval of boards with a hole in the middle, such as Basingstoke (see following section and picture). It needs about twice

Hawthorn Dene has two fiddle yards, each with five roads of varying lengths. The longer ones can hold two trains – for example, the leftmost one.

as many boards, which means it takes longer to set up, but it does allow the scenic boards to be wider. These layouts are usually operated from the centre, which means operators have to crawl under the boards – something that gets more difficult as the operator gets older.

LAYOUTS WITH JUNCTIONS

Things get really difficult if the scenic part contains a junction, so a train might come back on one of two different lines. Either both need to connect to one set of fiddle-yard roads, or each branch has a separate fiddle yard, and the lines join after the fiddle yard. Either way involves trains crossing those going in the other direction, so you

need to be careful to avoid crashes or blockages. If there is a lot of space you might be able to cross the other line by a flying or burrowing junction (as on Northallerton, shown at the start of the chapter), but the gradients will reduce the length of train the locos can haul.

Our previous club layout, Basingstoke, was particularly complex operationally. It had a four-track main line with a junction to an important two-track secondary route, and trains from both fast or slow lines could take the junction route junction. Some trains on the main line switched from fast to slow or vice versa. Many trains ought to have terminated and reversed, but operationally this was so difficult we rarely attempted it.

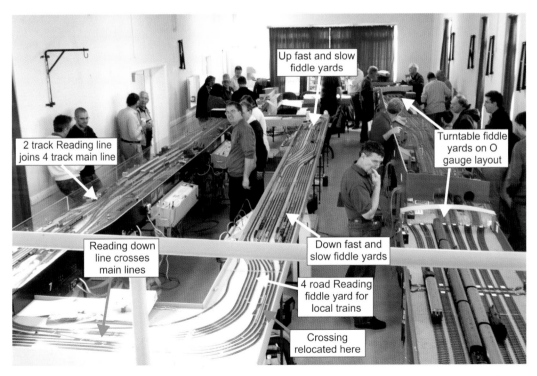

Basingstoke (N gauge) and Weydon Road (O) at a club open day. In the centre are the Basingstoke fiddle yards, the up fast and up slow yards at the far end, the down fast and down slow nearer the camera, and the small single-ended Reading fiddle yard nearest the camera. On the left of the picture six lines enter from the scenic part, four going to London at the bottom and two to Reading just above. The problem line is indicated with a red pointer. The down Reading trains have to cross the four-track main line, which can create a blockage, forcing a train to halt part-way off scene. We solved this by moving the crossing back to where the green arrow is. This left space between the crossing and the scenic area for a full-length train, so a train waiting for the crossing was clear of the scenic area. The O-gauge layout on the right shows the use of a turntable-style fiddle yard at each end.

We had four main operators: front and back, up and down. The back operators controlling the fiddle yards had much the more difficult task. Because the oval was a scale 2 miles long it took a train three minutes to go round. Since we aimed to keep trains moving, rather than have prototypical time gaps, a train had to be sent out before the previous one was back, and it was easy to get the fiddle-yard entry points wrong. Trains might not arrive back in the same order or on the same line, and the fiddle-yard operator had to be aware of this and swap them back before they entered the fiddle yard, otherwise one section would have too many trains.

What we learned is that if there are separate front and back operators, then each track that goes on or off scene must have space for a train to be held off scene. Trains are stopped there automatically until accepted by the receiving operator, so you can work out what to do with each train before it enters your part of the layout. Ideally there is detection of when the holding roads are full, and either an indicator light or the electrics prevent a second train being sent until the first is clear. The holding sections must be clear of any junctions within the fiddle yard.

OPERATING THE FIDDLE YARD AND AUTOMATION

With large numbers of trains of varying lengths it can be impossible to work out where to fit them. Avoid this problem by adopting the rule that each train is stored in a particular road and always goes back there after it has run round the layout.

You could drive every train into the fiddle yard and stop it in the correct position using the controller, but this is time-consuming and prone to error – if you get distracted it may continue on and crash, or get derailed on a point set against it.

If all the trains have the loco or powered coach of a multiple unit at the front, all that is needed to stop the train is a short isolated section at the front of each fiddle-yard road. A biased 'normally off' switch powers the section: you push it to release a train. It might at the same time set the exit point correctly. This can be done with DCC as well as with DC.

Double headers are a problem, as the front loco will stop while the second is still powered. If it is strong enough the second loco will push forwards until it is isolated as well; if not it will continue pushing against the front loco, which does it no good. You can make the rear loco an unpowered dummy, but the remaining one might not be able to haul the train; the better option is to run wires between the two locos to connect them electrically. This works with both DCC and DC, and improves electrical pick-up.

The isolation sections need to be long enough to ensure that all the locos stop before the end of the section. A heavy train can take several inches to stop if it is going fast.

With a multiple unit with the powered unit in the middle, or even worse at both front and back, a simple system of isolated sections will not work. You could isolate the whole road, and then turn it on for just long enough to move the train up to the correct position. However, a better option is to have train detection that turns the power off when the train gets to the front of the road.

More than one train can be stored in each road, perhaps two short trains or even several full-length trains. Manual operation works well for roads with two trains: the train stops in the back half of the road when it enters, and you push a button to move it forwards to the front half. However, with three or more trains manual operation is awkward and automation is desirable. It needs train detection: electronics to detect when a train is occupying a particular section. More complex layouts may need train recognition: being able to identify a particular train.

If a train always comes back before the next is sent out, the points at each end of the yard can be operated together so the same road is selected at each end.

More complex layouts will need to have two trains out at once – for example a stopper followed by an express that overtakes it in the station – and the points must be operated at each end independently. This is when operation gets really difficult: over several hours at an exhibition it is easy to put a train back in the wrong road and get in a muddle. This is another case where train recognition can simplify operation and avoid errors.

TRAIN DETECTION

The ability to detect trains is the basis for most automation. We installed it on Wickwar primarily to automate the fiddle yard, but we operate signals automatically as trains go past, illuminate LEDs on control panels to show the operator which sections are occupied, stop a second train being despatched when the scenic section is occupied, and prevent points being changed when a train is over them.

There are many methods of detecting trains. The simplest is to mount reed switches (small magnetically operated switches) or Hall-effect transistors (which detect a magnet) between the sleepers, and glue a magnet to each train. They are reliable, but only detect a train as it passes, so you may need another detector to know it has left the sector, and software to keep track of it. On the road system on Wickwar we detect the magnet on the Faller steering arm to operate a 'taxi rank', a queue of up to four vehicles that move up one place when the front one is despatched.

Optical detection has a beam of light that is interrupted by the train. The light source, an infra-red LED, can be mounted between the sleepers with the detector close by to detect light reflected off the underside of the train. Alternatively the light and detector can be on opposite sides of the train, angled to ensure they still detect the train when it stops with a gap between wagons next to the detector. Sunlight could cause interference: the better detectors modulate the light beam to avoid this.

My experience is that the positions of the light and detector need a lot of fiddling to get them totally reliable. You have to balance the sensitivity between reliably detecting different shapes of wagon and differently reflective undersides, and not detecting a hand nearby or a train on the adjacent track. If the light and detector are on opposite sides of the track, it has to register both a very low wagon such as a Weltrol, and one with big gaps underneath such as a bogie open.

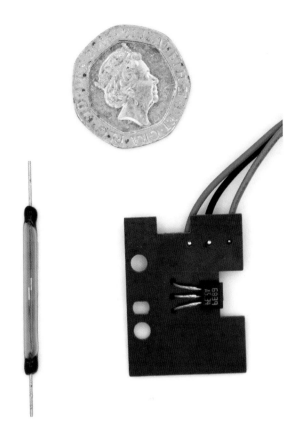

On the left is a reed switch of the common, normally open type, where the contacts are closed by a nearby magnet. A variant is a latching reed switch, which will open or close if the north or south pole of a magnet is waved nearby, and stay in that position. They are particularly useful for switching battery-powered lighting in coaches on and off; it can be done by a magnet positioned over the track as trains travel into and out of the scenic area. They are difficult to find, but Layouts4U stock them. On the right is a Hall-effect sensor, which detects a nearby magnetic field; it needs an electronics interface. It can distinguish between north and south poles: the Tomytec bus chassis uses one pole for stop/go and the other for fast/slow. Detection can be useful on automations to tell when a particular position has been reached.

Optical detectors need no modifications to train or track, and can detect all stock, not just locos. They register presence as long as any part of the train is over them. I've used the MERG Hector kits, built some of my own, and several commercial man-

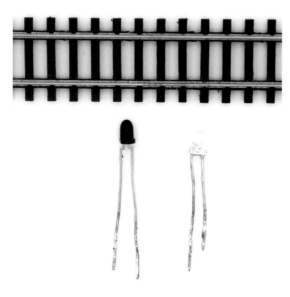

Infra-red emitters and detectors come in 3mm-diameter packages that will fit easily between sleepers. The associated electronics can be mounted under the board.

ufacturers can supply complete modules such as the Heathcote Irdot.

Train-on-track indicators (TOTI) detect the presence of a train anywhere within a whole section of track. The track is divided into sections with a permanent voltage across the two rails. Any stock within the section that conducts electricity causes a current flow, which is detected. For DCC systems there is always power on the track; for DC a low current voltage is added in parallel with the normal track power. It takes more work to install these than other systems since the track needs to be divided into sections with gaps and a separate wire to each section. Any motorized unit or a coach fitted with lights powered from the track will conduct and be detected, and a high-value resistor can be placed between the wheels on other stock so they can be detected. These are called 'resistive axles' and can be bought, or you can make your own.

On Wickwar we use TOTI with resistive axles at the end of each train. For reliability we found we

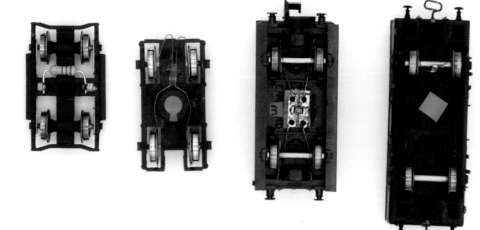

Various methods of adding a resistor across the wheels. From the left, a Dapol light-ready bogie only needs a resistor soldered between the pickups. Second, a normal coach bogie: a length of thin phosphor-bronze wire has been soldered to each side of a 0603 surface mount resistor and encased in epoxy for strength. It has been stuck to the top of the bogie and the wires bent so they touch the backs of the four wheels. Next, a similar arrangement under a wagon – in this case the resistor and wires are soldered to a scrap of strip board. All these work even if only a diagonally opposite pair of wheels are touching the track. Finally, a resistor glued to a wagon axle with the wires bent to touch the backs of the wheels. The latter is less reliable even with a pair of axles, as it only works with directly opposite wheels.

needed three at the end of each train, two in the last vehicle and one in an earlier one in case the last one derailed. A bonus is that if a train uncouples (far too common in N) it detects that the end of the train is still in the section and prevents the next train from running into it. We had to adjust the sensitivity of the detectors, and found that 5K resistors worked better than the 10K we started with.

TOTI is best installed from the start, as it needs a lot of wiring and section breaks. MERG sell kits for detectors that will work with DC or DCC. Ready-built detectors are available, and some DCC systems have them as an option.

TRAIN IDENTIFICATION

RFID (radio frequency identification) tags are small passive electronic circuits (no power supply) that can be put under rolling stock. A detector under the track transmits a radio wave that is used by the tag as a power source to transmit back a message containing its unique id. A computer such as a Raspberry Pi or Arduino is needed to process the codes.

They have the same limitations as magnetic detection, that it is only a passing indication. But train identification can be the basis for all sorts of further automation and can supplement other forms of train detection.

There are two main types of tag that you might use. Low-frequency tags (125kHz) cost a few pounds each and are relatively immune from interference from the metalwork. High-frequency tags (13.56MHz) cost tens of pence but work best if not directly mounted on metal.

Bar codes can be used. The codes can be printed off so they cost nothing, and readers are not expensive. However, standard bar codes are rather long to fit under N-gauge stock as they need white areas before and after as well as the code itself.

All are easy to add. The detectors go under the track and can read a few inches away. The tags or codes are glued under wagons.

Once you can recognize a train you can select the correct fiddle-yard road or route at a junction, or display information about the train to the public or the operator. We use low-frequency tags on the road system on Wickwar to identify vehicles, and display images of them on the operator's screen.

We use high-frequency tags to identify trains travelling south through Wickwar. The next signal box past Wickwar was a major junction where trains turned off on to the main GWR London–South Wales line. To indicate the route they expected to take they had to whistle as they passed through Wickwar: two for straight on, three if turning off. By detecting the train not only can we sound the correct whistle signal automatically, but we can choose the appropriate sound for the locomotive.

A high-frequency tag on the left, and two of the low-frequency glass-encapsulated tags on the right. Interface electronics and power supply are needed for the reader.

Wagon with HF tag stuck on between the body and the underframe.

WHISTLES AND HORN SIGNALS

Train whistles serve many purposes. They alert users when they are approaching a level crossing or a foot crossing. The whistle is sounded to warn men working on the track, or when entering or leaving a station if there is a train on the adjacent track. Trains that were double headed or had a banker used whistle codes to communicate between the drivers. When shunting, whistles were used to communicate with shunters or the signalman: for example, 'I am clear of the point, it is safe to change it.' When approaching a junction a whistle was used to indicate the expected route or to warn the signalman if the route seemed wrong. A coded whistle indicating the expected route would be given a block section prior to a major junction and passed to the signal box at the junction by a special 'train entering section' code.

The supplement to the working timetable had many pages detailing the different signals to be given. The use of whistles was very common, but radios mean they are much less used nowadays.

High-frequency tags or bar codes, being very cheap, can be used to identify individual wagons to automate shunting.

FIDDLE-YARD SHUFFLE AUTOMATION

If you want to store more than two trains per road, manual operation gets complex and prone to error. On complex layouts you might want to select the fiddle-yard road depending on the train approaching.

With train detection you can make the 'shuffling up' of trains happen automatically. Each fiddle-yard road is divided into several equal length sections. Power to a section is turned on if the section ahead is empty, so the train moves forwards into the empty section. Thus when a train is taken out of the front section the train behind moves up, then the one behind that, and so on. Provided you detect the ends of the trains, roads can hold a mix of long and short trains, with the long trains using two or more sections.

The automated shuffle on Wickwar has big advantages. It lets us hold a lot of trains in a small area. Instead of just six trains we have twenty-four. It is very easy to operate: you select one of the three roads and press a button to start the front train moving. By the time it has gone round the layout all the other trains have moved up, making space for it at the back of the road it came out of.

It took some time to get the shuffle working reliably, but now we can go for an entire day at an exhibition without a problem, perhaps 2,000 successful detections, and we no longer need an operator at all on the fiddle yard. It prevents fiddle-yard crashes: if a train stalls and fails to move up, the next train will not be able to enter the fiddle yard; similarly if part of a train uncouples.

If we were building a layout as complex as Basingstoke now, we would add train identification to route each train automatically to the correct road of the fiddle yard.

The fiddle yard on Wickwar has three roads in each direction, each divided into four to six sections. An automated shuffle moves trains up to the front of each road. Each section is labelled (for example, E4) to show where trains go when loading stock before an exhibition. When the track leaves the scenic area there is plain track round the curve so there is always space for a train to go off scene. The fiddle yard goes along the back and continues round the curve at the far end. Using the curve almost doubles its capacity.

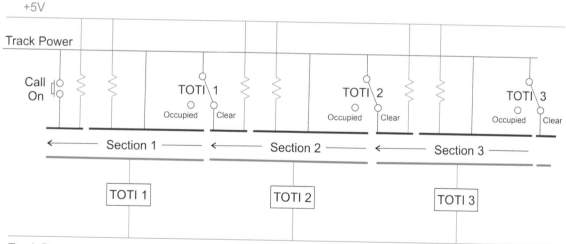

The diagram shows one road of the Wickwar fiddle yard with trains going right to left. The shuffle uses a MERG train-on-track indicator (TOTI) on each fiddle-yard section. If a section is occupied, a short length of track at the front of the section behind is isolated. When the section becomes clear the power is switched on to the section in the rear so a train moves up. It operates in the same way for both DC and DCC. The 5V supply via a resistor provides a current flow that can be detected if the section is isolated from the track power, or for DC if the controller is turned off.

CHAPTER FIVE

TRACK AND WIRING

TRACK

TERMINOLOGY

'Points': This is the term used by modellers in the UK and by most railwaymen, though permanent way engineers refer to them as 'turnouts', and in the USA they are referred to as 'turnouts' or 'switches'.

Tie bar: This joins the ends of the two blades together, and is moved in order to change the direction in which the turnout is set. It is a modeller's term; the rough equivalent on a real point is called a stretcher bar, rod, or gauge rod.

POINT SIZES

Point sizes (on the real railway) are specified by a letter and a number: the letter indicates the length of the point blade, the shortest being 'A' (9ft, 2.75m), going up to 'F' (30ft, 9m). The number is the angle of the crossing, so a B8 has a 1-in-8 crossing angle. Longer blades tend to go with higher-numbered (shallower) crossing angles. The combinations where the switch blade and closure rail are the same curvature are known as 'natural turnouts', and are preferred: A7, B8, C10, D12, F16. For shorter crossings, such as A5, A6 and B7, the closure rail has a tighter curve, and for longer ones part of the closure rail is straight.

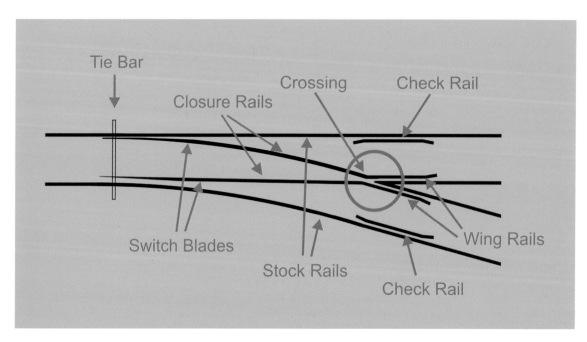

Stock rails are the continuous rails on each side of the point. A crossing or V is where the rails cross each other; modellers often refer to it as the 'frog', the term used in the USA. A check rail is a rail inside the stock rail to force the wheel hard up against the stock rail alongside the crossing (they are also found on tight curves). 'Switch blades' are the moving part, and 'closure rails' the fixed rails from the blade to the crossing. 'Wing rails' are their extension beyond the crossing, and act as another check rail.

'A'-size crossings are rare except where space is very tight in sidings; the GWR did not use them at all. 'B' is fairly common in sidings, while 'C' would be common on running lines in steam days. Even a 'C' crossing would have speed restrictions, which would be more severe for trains taking the diverging route, or if it were a facing crossing. For high-speed running much longer points are needed, and for very high speeds, and angles that are less than 1-in-30, a 'swing nose' design is used, where the wing rails move so there is no gap at the crossing.

If two points are used together for a crossover they must have the same crossing angle; similarly any associated diamonds crossings must have the same angle.

Peco points all have the same crossing angle so they all fit together, but they do not correspond to any prototype size. Peco large radius points are close to B6 size, medium are close to A5, and small would only be found in a dockyard or light railway with locos with a very short wheelbase.

On the scenic part of the layout use the longest points you can as they look more realistic.

GRADIENTS

If a track goes on a bridge over another line, gradients can't be avoided. However, gentle gradients such as 1 in 200 can be modelled as level track without it looking wrong. The downside of gradients is that they limit the length of trains you can haul, which

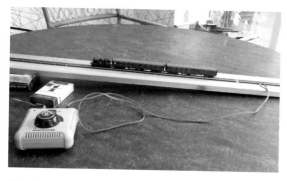

Check your planned gradient with a length of track on an inclined plank to see what your locos can pull. If the gradient is on a curve it will restrict even more the size of load a train can pull.

may not be an issue for a branch line with short trains, but can be a problem for full-length trains on a main line. Gradients on models are often steeper than the prototype because the track length has been compressed. If you plan to include gradients, first check what your locos can pull.

Where the gradient changes, make it gradual, spread over at least 6in (15cm). A sharp change in gradient at the start of an incline means a loco could be supported just by the outer wheels, which on many steam locos are not driven, so it will stall. Abrupt changes in slope also cause uncoupling and derailments.

PECO TRACK

The vast majority of N-gauge layouts use Peco track. There is a choice between code 55 and code 80, but code 55 looks far better than code 80.

A second reason for choosing code 55 is that it is much more robust than code 80. This is because it is really code 80 track with the bottom third of the rail buried in the plastic sleepers. It is far stronger than the small chairs holding code 80 rail. If you catch the end of the rail at the edge of the baseboard with your clothing, as is easy to do when putting up a board, code 80 rail pulls out of the sleepers and needs replacing, while code 55 rips your clothing. For code 80 it is advisable to solder the rail to PCB or to brass screws for strength, while code 55 is fine just glued in place.

Use electrical frog rather than insulated frog points. Wiring them up is not difficult (despite what some people say), and you get better running because they do not have a dead section of plastic with no pick-up for the loco.

Code 55 only comes as flexible track, while code 80 has both flexible and set-track (fixed shape). Laying flexible track is easy except for tight curves, where it is difficult to get a uniform curve. Sections can end up slightly tight, and that is where your stock is likely to derail or uncouple. It helps to bend the track to a tighter curve before laying it, then let it relax to the curve you want. It is best to use Track-Setta curves – strips of steel of varying radii that fit between the rails to get the curve exact

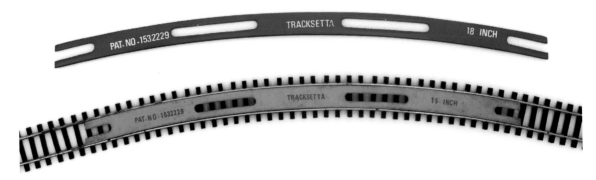

A variety of sizes of 'Track-Setta' gauges – these are strongly recommended for laying curves in flexible track of 15in (38cm) radius or less. They are available in 3in (7.5cm) steps from 9in (23cm) up to 24in (60cm), plus a few larger ones; the 12in (30cm) and 15in are probably the most useful.

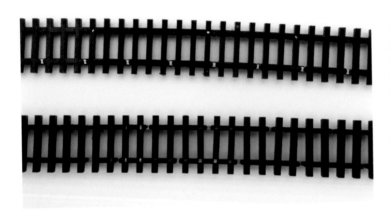

While code 80 flexible track can be bent either way, there is a preferred direction for code 55. At the top is code 55, with all gaps in the web between sleepers at the bottom: it should be curved with the gaps on the inside. Below is code 80, where the gaps alternate sides. Having the gaps all on one side means the sleepers are more evenly spaced on sharp curves.

Joining code 80 (left) and 55 (right) is easy: the fishplate fits on the second foot of the code 55 rail, which is normally buried in the sleepers. The rail heights are almost the same overall – code 55 is very slightly higher. Pack under the sleepers of the code 55 next to the joint: 0.30in (0.75mm) plasticard is about right.

while you pin it down. If you are a member of a model railway club you may be able to borrow them.

Try to avoid isolation gaps on flexible track curves – the rail tends to straighten where cut, so you get a kink and possible derailments. If you have to, put panel pins on the outside of the rail and solder the rail to them.

Because of the difficulty of getting perfect tight curves, I prefer to use code 80 and set-track curves in the non-scenic areas, and code 55 for the scenic parts.

It is good practice to include 'transition curves': rather than going from straight track to a tight curve, have a few inches of a curve of larger radius between the two. It is not essential, but it will give smoother running.

FINETRAX – AN ALTERNATIVE TO PECO

While well weathered Peco code 55 looks good, it is not ideal. The depth and width of the rail is slightly over-scale, there is no gap between sleepers and rail, and it has a web between sleepers to hide the downward extension of the rail. The sleeper spacing is correct for 1:160 scale, so too close for 1:148 scale. The sleepers are too deep, but because they will be covered in ballast this only matters if they are used as a wagon load.

The points are the least satisfactory part of Peco code 55 track. The appearance suffers because the switch blades of code 55 points are code 80 – the sleepers in the centre of the point are lower than elsewhere to accommodate them.

The gaps between rails at the crossing are designed to accommodate 1980s N-gauge wheels made to much coarser standards than the modern NMRA wheels. The NMRA standards specify a gap of 0.7mm for points: Peco points are 1.2mm. At the tip of the crossing the actual gap is twice this, about 2.4mm, and since NMRA wheels are only 1.8mm wide, they can drop into the gap as they go over. If you watch a rake of modern four-wheel wagons passing slowly over a Peco point you will see each one lurch as the wheel drops into the gap.

If you want something better, look at the FineTrax range of track and point kits. It is code 40 rail (the correct scale for heavier rail), the correct sleeper spacing for UK track, and the rail is clear of the sleepers with minimal web between sleepers. The gaps on the points, while larger than true scale, are much smaller than Peco and close to NMRA standards, so look better and give smooth running with modern wheels. The downside is they are kits, so it is more work.

Plain track is easy. Lengths of rail, and moulded plastic sleepers in blocks of four are available, and you just thread the sleepers on to the rail. The company sells a jig to help, but I find it easy enough without – you could do many yards of track while watching a television programme.

Even if you don't adopt FineTrax generally, there are a couple of places you might use the plain track.

The main track is Peco code 55, but the siding is FineTrax with its lighter rail. Note that fishplates are not used with FineTrax: the rails are simply lined up and the sleepers pinned or glued down.

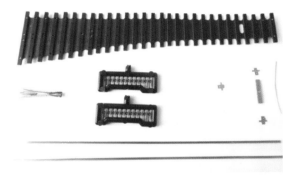

FineTrax point kit. The kit contains a base plate for the size of point being built, with holes into which you fit moulded chairs with pins on the bottom.

The first is for track panels loaded on a wagon, where the scale-thickness sleepers and finer rail look much better. The second is to use a length of FineTrax for a siding, as these are often old track with lighter rail than the newer running lines, and it gives this difference in size.

Building FineTrax points is more effort, but does not require great skills. After the first few you will be able to make one in a couple of hours.

There are three types of chair: plain chairs, check-rail chairs (double chairs that hold the check rail as well), and slide chairs with no inside chair for where the switch-rail tip goes close to the stock rail. The instructions make it clear which chairs are needed where. The chairs have an inside and an outside, and they need to be the right way round to line up properly.

The switch rail has to be cut to length and then filed at one end to create the thin blade. There is a jig for this, and unless you have built points before I suggest you use it. You don't want to file too much away or the blade will be too flexible; if it is not right, throw it away and start again: rail is cheap. You have to solder a plate and pin on to the end of the blade; the jig for filing the blades includes one to help solder the plate on. The plate fits under the stock rail and keeps the blade flat; the pin fits into a pre-drilled tie bar, which is supplied. It is not difficult provided you don't use too much solder; it is easiest using solder paste. Wash thoroughly afterwards to get rid of any remaining flux, which otherwise over time may turn the metal green.

The crossing is a separate casting that is mounted directly on to the point base.

The kit produces a point that should work perfectly first time, with no need for gauges.

Electrical connections need soldering on. Most are best done before threading the rail through the chairs. I use short lengths of stiff tinned copper wire going vertically down. You need a connection to each stock rail, each point blade, and the crossing itself. There are two short lengths of rail past the crossing. Leave these out when building the point and extend the rail of the adjacent plain track to go through these chairs when you lay it.

The wires to the point blades are connected directly to the adjacent stock rail. This ensures that the blades are always the same polarity as the adjacent stock rail, so it removes the possibility of a short if a wheel back touches the adjacent open point blade: this is particularly important with DCC. It means the extremely large gap on Peco points to avoid this can be reduced to something more realistic. You need to switch the power to the crossing, usually by a micro-switch mounted on the point motor. It gives more reliable operation than relying on point blades making contact: I wire Peco points this way as well.

Finally, glue the chairs to the base using Butanone. The pins under the chairs are such a tight fit that the point stays together well without glue while you are building it.

FineTrax is finer than Peco, but that means it is less robust. It is still fairly strong, but for example is more easily damaged if something heavy is dropped on it. So take a little more care, and perhaps use a gentler point motor than a Peco solenoid.

FineTrax is available with wood sleepers and bullhead rail, or concrete sleepers and flat-bottomed rail. It has modern concrete sleeper points with flat-bottom rail: this type of point has become common in the twenty-first century. Three sizes are currently available, left- or right-handed: AV7 (slightly smaller than Peco long) typically found in a siding where space is tight, CV10 for a siding or low speed crossover, and EV15 for a turnout taken at speed.

A completed B6 FineTrax point at the top, with a Peco long point at the bottom for comparison.

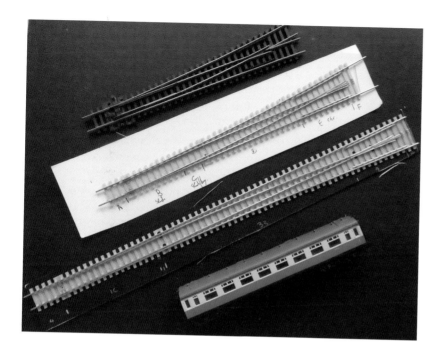

Top to bottom: *A Peco long turnout, FineTrax CV10 turnout, EV15 turnout, and a coach for comparison.*

The EV15 turnouts would really stand out on a modern layout featuring a junction and little else. Though it seems very long, it is still short compared with turnouts designed for 100mph (160km/h) running, which can be more than twice the length.

ADJUSTING WHEEL BACK-TO-BACKS

If wagons run poorly through points, or derail, this may be because the distance between the backs of the wheels – the back-to-back (BtB) – is wrong. Modern wheels are set to a BtB of 7.40–7.55mm, while older wheels were set to 7.20mm. These still work, but a BtB of less than 7.20mm can cause problems, particularly on Peco diamond crossings and slips. I try to set all my wheels to about 7.5mm, as this generally improves running. The larger BtB reduces the amount a wagon can twist on the track, so it runs straighter, which helps on points. Too small a BtB can often be the reason that pony trucks on locos derail.

Adjust the back-to-back of wheels. If they are too close together insert two pairs of fine-nosed pliers as shown, then gently lever one against the other to open out the wheels a little. If they are too far apart, put a small nut (say, 8BA) over each pin-point, and then squeeze them together in a vice until you have the correct spacing.

You can buy back-to-back gauges, but many are for the old 7.2mm standard so are not much use. It is easier to use digital callipers.

IMPROVING RUNNING THROUGH PECO SLIPS

The crossing gaps on Peco slips are particularly large. This can cause stock to take the wrong route through the crossing, leading to derailments, or even occasionally to turn off on to the other track!

The red line shows the large gap, which is too wide and long because the rail that ends in a point on the right of the gap is too short: if it were 2 or 3mm longer it would support the wheel properly, as shown by the red line at the top.

The solution: a strip of nickel-silver sheet soldered to the outside of the rail, protruding about 2.5mm further, and bent slightly. It sounds more difficult than it is: I managed to do it with the slip in place on the layout.

If you have this problem, and adjusting back-to-backs does not cure it, the best solution is to modify the crossing to reduce the size of the gap. Find a piece of 10 thou (0.25mm) thick nickel silver – for those who have ever built any etched nickel-silver kits, the scrap etch will provide plenty. Cut four rectangles 1.2mm high and 13mm long (cut them oversize and file them down). This is for code 55 track; code 80 probably needs them more than 1.2mm deep. Bend a very shallow angle 3.5mm from the end. Clean the etch and the outside of the rail where it is to go with a glassfibre brush. Coat the inside of the rectangle with solder paste.

Put the rectangle in place with tweezers, and hold it with a small bulldog clip at the end away from the crossing, as shown in the picture. Check that the end of the rectangle is just short of where there is a break in the adjacent rail. Apply a soldering iron to the top of the rail for a few seconds: the solder paste will melt and form a shiny surface.

Provided you work quickly and have the iron at, say, 360°C, the slip will not suffer any heat damage. Remove the clip and check that the rectangle is securely attached; if it is not, repeat. Do the same for the other three similar positions. Take a small file and go over the top of the rectangles to make the tops level with the rail head. Your stock should now run through much better.

The rectangle ready to be soldered in place.

GAPS BETWEEN TRACKS

Peco track is designed so that a crossover – whichever points are being used – gives a gap between the tracks (measured between rails) of a scale of about 8ft 6in (2.6m). On the prototype, the gap between two running lines is usually only the minimum allowed of 6ft (1.8m), though it can be more. The gap between a running line and a passing loop or siding must be at least 10ft (3m), and there must be a gap at least this big on one side or the other of every running line, for safety. So the Peco gap is a compromise. It has to be at least the size it is on typical N-gauge curves to prevent passing coaches hitting each other. However, if there are only large-radius curves in the scenic areas the gaps can be smaller.

Gaps closer to scale and of varying size give an extra air of realism to the track, particularly viewed from a distance, as N-gauge track usually is. If using FineTrax, adjusting the spacing is no problem, but Peco points need modifying to fit closer together. You need to cut off about 16mm of rail from the end of the stock (outer) rail beyond the crossing on both points, and remove the outer halves of the two sleepers under the rail. They can then be positioned so the gap is much less – about a scale 7ft (2.1m).

After putting track in place, and before gluing it down by ballasting, check that the gaps are big enough by putting one of your longest coaches on each track and checking they do not knock against each other as you push them past each other.

PAINTING/WEATHERING TRACK

The biggest improvement you can make to the appearance of your track is to paint the side of the rails a dark brown 'track dirt' colour. They are never shiny metal, and almost never have bright orange

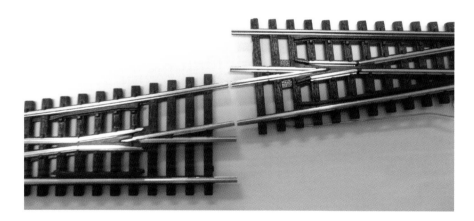

Top: *A pair of Peco points as a crossover showing the standard 17mm gap.* **Below:** *With the rails cut back to reduce the gap between tracks to 14mm.*

Well weathered track on Stoney Lane Depot. Track in yards often had old or inferior ballast and was not maintained and replaced regularly, as were running tracks.

rust: even very new rail is a dark rust. Leaving code 55 shiny, or painting it orange, emphasizes that it is a little over-scale.

The ballast is often stained dark brown, particularly between the rails, and always in platforms and other places where trains stand up.

The parts of the crossing the wheels don't run over should be dark brown; chemical blackening is better than paint. Polish the blackening off the running surface so this is bright, leaving the tops of the wing rails brown. Check rails can be treated in the same way (if metal), or painted brown.

POINT RODDING

As a final touch you can add point rodding, the bars that run from the signal box to operate the

The fast way to paint the rails is using an air brush: to paint the rail sides hold them close to horizontal, and vertically to paint between them. Immediately clean the top and the inside corner of the rail with a cloth dampened with thinners, because trains will not pick up from a painted rail. I recommend doing this before adding scenery, though it is possible to do so afterwards, as shown!

Point rodding formed from guitar wire (0.2mm diameter) and etched stools. Other details in this picture are the barrow crossing, formed from stained matchsticks; the warning signs printed on a laser printer; and the small (prototypical) cut-away in the platform edge to provide clearance for locos going over the crossing.

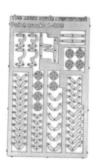

Less effort and almost as good looking are etches of groups of rods from the 2mm Scale Association (only available to members). They have seven rods next to each other. Cut down to the number you need, and solder on a detail etch (alongside, top) to represent the stools, as has been done for the top two. The other etch is of various cranks, which can be used with either the wire or etched rodding.

Rodding next to the signal box from 2mm Scale Association etched rodding. Note the cranks to change direction through 90 degrees. 'Compensators' were put in the middle of runs to change from push to pull, so that half the rod would be pulling and half pushing, cancelling out any thermal expansion.

points. Unless they are close to the front of the layout people are unlikely to notice them, but they do show up in photos of the track, and are particularly noticeable by the signal box, where there may be dozens of them.

The booklet *Point Rodding – Prototype and Planning Notes for Modellers* from the 2mm Scale Association gives more information.

WIRING AND OPERATION

WIRING

While new fishplates conduct current well, over time they tend to corrode, and after five years of being stored in a basement – as many exhibition layouts are – they can stop conducting properly and there is increased resistance or a section of dead track. Squeezing the fishplate with pliers will usually fix it for a little while, or in extremis removing the rail and cleaning it or soldering the fishplate. I prefer to avoid the problem by having a dropper wire from every section of rail to below the baseboard, not relying on the fishplates at all.

Dropper wires are best soldered to the underside of the rail before laying the track, then they will be invisible once ballasted. I use solid tinned 28 SWG copper wire for the droppers so I don't have to worry about stray strands: they are never going to be moved once laid, so the extra flexibility of multi-core cable is not needed. Some modellers solder wires to the underside of the fishplates, but I don't like this as it relies on the fishplates continuing to conduct to the rail.

When laying the track, note where the dropper is, and drill a small hole for it through the baseboard. Connect them up with standard multicore cable under the baseboard. Once ballasted the dropper will be completely invisible.

It is good practice to put insulating fishplates between the rails where there is an isolation gap. This is not to hold the rail in line – the isolating fishplates are fairly useless for this – but to prevent the rails moving and closing the isolation gap. Temperature changes cause this, for example going from a cold garage to a hot exhibition. If it is not convenient to add an insulating fishplate – and many gaps are cut after laying the track – a two-part

Cut about a 3in (8cm) length of wire, bend the end 2mm at right angles, and tin. Clean the underside of the rail, either at the end or in a gap between sleepers, and solder on the dropper. It is easier if you use some flux, though wash the residue off afterwards if you do. Provided you are reasonably fast you will not damage the plastic when soldering.

epoxy glue applied to the gap and the outside of the rail will provide an insulating barrier. Make sure it does not protrude on the top or the inside of the rail, otherwise running will suffer.

DCC OR DC?

You probably have your own views as to which of these you prefer. As the years progress DCC is increasingly the standard. I strongly prefer DCC for small layouts such as a terminus, and it is a clear winner for an engine shed or MPD, but for a simple through station the advantages are less obvious.

Some advantages of DCC come from being able to configure the chip in the loco to the motor to improve running, and to make all locos run at similar speeds on the same throttle setting. Even more of an advantage is the use of pulse wave modulation (PWM) to drive the motor, rather than pure DC. This gives much better slow speed control. PWM controllers are available for DC, but most people use a more basic controller. Some DCC chips allow for a 'keep alive' capacitor, which acts as an electronic flywheel to help prevent stalling. All these together mean that far better slow speed running can be achieved under DCC, particularly important for shunting.

The main reduction in wiring with DCC is because there are no isolation sections. How important this is depends on the layout. Wickwar has no isolation sections even for DC, as all trains run through, possibly stopping at the station. The few that shunt the goods yard need access to all tracks (both lines) because of the track layout. On the other hand, a layout based on an engine shed needs an isolation section every few inches. If you want to model banking, DCC makes that easier; train-on-track detection may require separately wired track sections whether DCC or DC.

Apart from cost, one of the few disadvantages of DCC over DC is that to control a loco you first need to identify the loco and its DCC address. This is no problem on a small layout with two or three locos, but on a big layout with dozens of trains in the fiddle yard it can be an issue. You can use a computer to track trains and perhaps be the throttle, but that is a lot of complication. On Wickwar we just set all trains to run at a sensible speed, and stop them in the fiddle yard by isolating the section they are on. We take the next train from the fiddle yard by turning its section on. We only need to know loco numbers for the two or three that stop at the station.

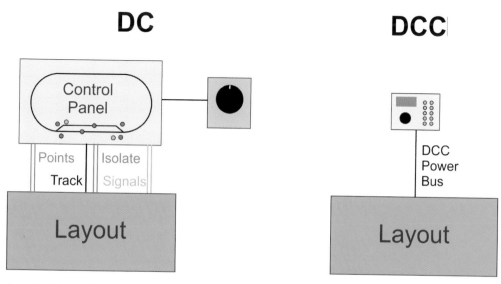

A typical simple DC system on the left, contrasted with a basic DCC system on the right. The big reduction in wiring is partly at the expense of the loss of a control panel, which is easier to use than buttons on the DCC controller. Adding one to the DCC system will add wiring.

The saving by not having point and signal wiring is at the expense of a control panel. For any except the smallest layout this is undesirable, and for a large layout it is unworkable. A control panel can be added to a DCC system, but this is not part of the basic DCC specification and involves more wiring and/or hardware. Control panels are dealt with in a later section.

POINT MOTORS

There are many types of point motor. The Peco solenoid motors are cheap and reliable. They are best powered by a capacitor discharge unit (CDU), which gives a large pulse of power. CDUs are available from most model shops, or you can build your own. They are usually operated by a probe that you touch to a contact on a track diagram. By using diodes, a 'diode matrix', one stud can set all the points on a route.

Solenoids are noisy and brutal, slamming the tie bar across hard, and after years of exhibition use a few tie bars might break and the points need replacing. This started happening on Basingstoke but only after ten years with a few heavily used Peco points, so it is not a big worry. Hand-built track might be more delicate.

Two other popular point motors, Tortoise and Cobalt, use a motor that moves the tie bar more slowly and gently, though they are more expensive. Cobalt point motors are available with analogue control or a built-in DCC interface. They both have built-in switches for powering the point crossing.

My preference is to use a servo motor. As well as the motor you need a mounting and electronics

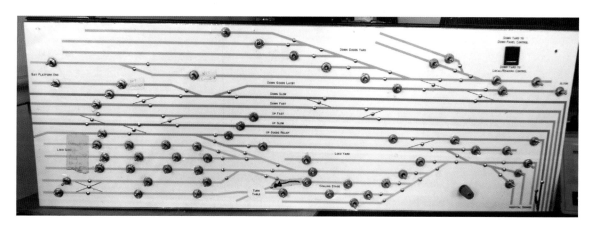

One of the six control panels on Basingstoke; it uses Peco solenoid motors. Routes are set by touching a probe plugged into the red CDU socket on the right to one of the studs on the panel, which connect via diode matrices to the points. The switches operate isolation sections.

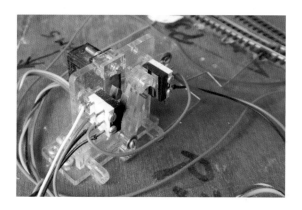

A servo on Wickwar mounted above the board in the fiddle yard using a MERG servo mount. The same mounting is used below the baseboard for points in the scenic area. Four micro-switches provide switching of the point crossing: you could manage with two, but four are easier to position correctly. The 'Omega loop' in the operating wire absorbs any excess movement of the wire without damaging the tie bar.

to power the servo. You can make your own servo mounts, or a number of companies such as Mega Point Controllers sell them. One advantage of a commercial mount is that it provides for mounting micro-switches to switch current to the point crossing. Drivers for servos are widely available, and come with a variety of interfaces so they can connect directly to a switch or to various bus systems, including DCC. I use kits from MERG (Model Electronics Railway Group) that are cheap and flexible.

The same servo motors and control electronics can be used to power many other things on the layout such as semaphore signals, level crossings, stops on a Faller roadway, and animations.

CONTROL PANELS AND LAYOUT CONTROL BUS

Much the easiest way to control the setting of points and signals is by using a control panel with a track diagram and switches or push buttons in appropriate places – this is called a mimic panel. LEDs can be added to show which route is set. For DC systems it will have isolation section switches as well. A good way to make a panel is from a box with a lid of clear

plastic sheet. Mount switches in holes on the lid, and place a printed track diagram behind it.

An alternative to a physical control panel is to display one on a touch screen and use this to control the layout. JMRI (jmri.org) provides tools for creating control panels and linking them to your layout electronics.

A large layout will have control panels in several places, each controlling points and so on, on several boards.

While the DCC track feed can connect the points as well, it is not suitable for connecting additional controllers or control panels. As a result many DCC manufacturers have added a second proprietary network called a throttle network, whose primary function is to connect additional handsets (throttles). Digitrax developed LocoNet on top of Ethernet protocols, and it has been adopted by several other manufacturers, including Fleischmann and Piko. These networks often allow control panels to be connected as well.

In 2016 the NMRA issued a specification for layout command control (LCC) with CAN Bus as the network, though it can link with proprietary throttle networks. CAN Bus is a network devel-

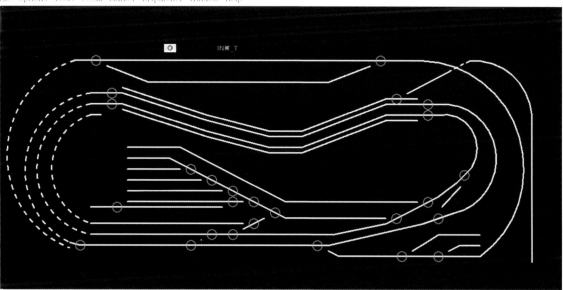

A control panel on a computer screen, drawn using JMRI software.

oped by the automotive industry for use in cars. It is designed to work in a difficult environment, and controller chips are widely available.

Little hardware for LCC is currently available, but it is sure to grow in popularity. However, MERG have their own layout bus CBUS, based on CAN Bus. Over twenty kits are available, including point drivers for most types of motor.

Both LCC and CBUS are systems for connecting together control panels, controllers, turnouts, signals, train detection, and anything else electrical on or off the layout. They are not tied to any particular train-control system and can be used with both DC and DCC – as indeed we do on Wickwar.

Apart from reducing wiring, a layout bus has many other advantages. You can have multiple control panels and complete flexibility over what is on each panel. When starting to operate a new layout you often realize that your original control-panel layout could be improved. This is easy with a bus, as the wiring to the panel is unchanged.

CBUS can be configured to link events, so a push button might change several points to set a route, or a train-on-track detector might be told to light a particular LED on a panel.

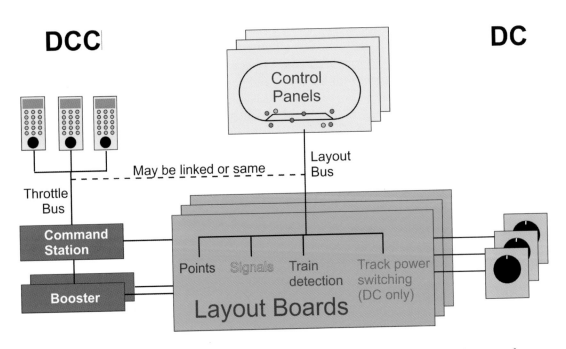

With a layout bus, no other wires are needed between control panels and the layout boards except for train control. It can be used with DCC, on the left, or DC, on the right. DCC power boosters (shown) isolate areas of track so a short on one does not stop operation on the rest of the layout – any large layout should use them. The layout bus can double as the throttle bus, or be linked, or be completely separate. For DC, additional network devices will be needed on the layout to switch power to sections of track, either to isolate them or to change controller.

CHAPTER SIX

SCENERY AND BACKSCENES

SCENERY

I've tried many ways of forming scenery. The one I recommend is to use a base of foam sculpted to shape and covered with a layer of a plaster mix called Sculptamold, which forms a hard surface. It is simple, versatile, lightweight, and extremely strong and robust: Wickwar has travelled to many exhibitions without any damage. Other methods I have tried, such as plaster bandages or paper plus plaster over cardboard, have come loose over time, as well as being heavier and not as simple.

The base of the scenery is hard foam. The best is Styrofoam, but the most convenient are sheets of insulation foam from DIY shops. There are many different types, but you want the sort that is very hard, and difficult to push your thumb into. You don't want the silver foil on the outside, but it is easy to peel it off. To stick it to the baseboard, or to stick two sheets together, use 'Insta Stick' foam adhesive,

> **PRACTISE FIRST!**
>
> Don't try out new techniques on your layout: practise away from the layout until you can get the effect you want. Don't be put off trying something new because it may not work – try it out on a scrap of ply or foam. For weathering, practise on old or damaged items.

available from DIY and tool shops. It is extremely strong, and sticks to almost anything, including skin (so use gloves). The foam must be held in place for a few minutes until the glue stops foaming and expanding. The glue fills substantial gaps and dries fairly hard. When you have finished, let a blob come out of the top of the tube and harden; this will keep the remainder usable for several months.

Wickwar under construction. The yellow foam has been sculpted to shape with a knife, most of it covered in Sculptamold (white areas), then painted dark brown. The foreground has a first layer of static grass. The hotel is a rough mock-up, photos pasted on to a block of foam that only took about forty minutes to make.

Wickwar at an earlier stage of construction, with the blocks of foam in place, but still to be sculpted. On the right is the ply edge of the board, still to be cut down to the level of the field.

Thin ply is needed on the outer edges to protect the foam from damage. When making the base-boards, put ply on the edges higher than the highest scenery, then cut it to the required profile when you shape the scenery.

To shape the foam, I use a long-bladed knife – the type with snap-off blades with the blade fully extended is ideal – then finish with coarse sandpaper. An 'oscillating tool' with a vibrating saw blade can be used for the initial shaping and to shape the ply at the edges at the same time.

A 3lb bag of Sculptamold will cover up to 1sq m (10sq ft) of foam. The layer need only be 2mm thick. Mix about a third of a mug at a time, kneading it well to get lumps out. The mix must be fairly dry, otherwise it takes much longer to set. It has a lumpy finish when applied, which is fine for rough moorland. It can be smoothed with a palette knife dipped in clean water, or a wet finger or paintbrush. If you want a very flat surface, sand it down after it has dried. Rocks (or cork or plaster 'rocks') can be embedded by pressing them in while the Sculptamold is damp. Wash out the mug after each batch: it will stick if it dries, and it is not good to mix the part-set remains with the new mix. If you are not happy with the contours you can go back and add another layer.

Sculptamold is a mix of wood fibre, clay and plaster sold by art shops and some model shops. When mixed with water it can be spread over foam, wood, or almost any other material to form a hard surface. It sticks tenaciously to almost everything, even clean glass. It dries hard but not brittle, and can be drilled and sanded once dry. The plaster can settle out at the bottom of the bag, so invert it and give it a good shake before use. After use, fasten the bag tightly: if the contents get damp they will not set properly.

Once you have the surface you want, paint it brown or green in case bare patches show through the 'grass'. We used Sandtex ultra-smooth 'bitter chocolate' colour masonry paint. A tester pot was enough for 2sq m (20sq ft) of boards. We allowed a few days for it to dry out fully before painting.

It is possible to mix powdered paint into the mix instead, but a lot is needed and we found it easier to paint it afterwards.

STATIC GRASS

At one time coloured scatter, similar to sawdust, was used to represent grass, but now static grass is preferred. Static grass consists of short, coloured fibres and is available in a range of colours and lengths. It is applied using a 'static grass applicator'. A layer of water-based glue (PVA) is put on the area to be grassed, and a wire from the static grass applicator is connected to the glue, typically clipped to a pin within the area. The grass is put in the applicator, then shaken on to the layout. The applicator will have charged it with static electricity so it stands up vertically. For small areas puff bottles can be used, though they do not create as much static.

There are a number of suppliers of applicators and static grass. One of the largest ranges is WWScenics; their products are distributed by Peco. They have grass in 1mm, 2mm, 4mm and 6mm lengths. You can get longer, but for N-gauge 6mm represents tall meadow grass, and it is unlikely you will want taller. They have twenty-five different colours of 2mm grass, and it is a good idea to have a selection of colours so you can vary them. For example, in well-watered areas with good soil the grass will be greener. If you need to match colours to those on a backscene it is even more important to have a range of colours.

WWScenics sells a layering spray, which allows you to add a second layer, usually of longer grass, over the first, and indeed a third and fourth layer. This is useful if you want to adjust the colour by adding a little of a lighter or darker grass colour.

There are many makers of static grass applicators, with considerable variation in price. You can even make your own from an electric fly swat, or buy something very similar on eBay. The more expensive ones cover large areas more quickly.

There are many demonstrations of techniques on the internet.

TREES

A variety of well-modelled trees, each with its own character, will enhance a layout, particularly if positioned near the front. Trees are useful near the backscene: they help blend it in and disguise the transition. A removable tree can conceal a board join. Commercially available trees vary from cheap 'bottle-brush' examples best reserved for Christmas cake decoration, to exquisite hand-made trees. However, really good trees are expensive.

The starter pack from WWScenics contains everything you need to begin. After trials you may want to buy other different colours and lengths of static grass to suit what you are modelling.

TREES

There is enormous variety in the size, shape and colour of trees – much more than people realize until they look at them closely. The shape mainly depends on the species, but individual trees also vary a lot. Fully grown trees of the larger species are enormous – a fully grown oak or ash is three or four times the height of a house. Near buildings trees are cut back, but are still usually higher than the buildings. The trees on most layouts are far too small – in fact some trees that are sold as suitable for O are about the right size for a large tree in N.

The copper wires from welding cable are twisted together to form the trunk, then split out into smaller bundles to form branches, getting steadily thinner. Alongside is Woodland Scenics Poly Fibre: this can be teased out until it is very thin, and glued on to represent twigs.

Some of the basic materials. A metre of welding cable doesn't cost much and provides plenty of fine wires; alternatively old car battery leads can be used. For dead or thicker branches, florist's wire can be used, which is paper-covered so easier to glue. A length of thicker wire in the centre of the trunk provides a spike for fixing the tree to the baseboard. The window sealant is to cover the trunk. The branches are sprayed with cheap hair fixer to stick on coloured flock for leaves.

I like to make my own trees, always working from a photo of a particular tree. The basic structure consists of an armature of twisted fine copper wire with window sealant applied over the trunk, then painted.

There are alternatives for the armature/trunk. Sea foam looks good and is simple, but it breaks easily – I would only use it for places where it is not likely to get caught by operators, for example next to the backscene. Sagebrush is even better, with a more realistic trunk, but difficult to get in the UK. Taller 'leafless trees' can be used as armatures, and other companies sell plastic armatures that are cheaper but less realistic.

The above is only an outline. For those who want to make trees I advise acquiring one or more of Gordon Gravett's excellent books; alternatively invite someone to demonstrate the techniques at a model railway exhibition or club.

Spread sealant over the trunk and thicker branches. Brown window sealant works well and doesn't show up if any fails to get painted. Paint the armature, noting that most trunks are more grey than brown. Add the polyfibre, and finally the flock. Examples of trees made in this way can be seen in the photographs of Wickwar in this book.

HEDGES

Much the same techniques can be used for hedges as for trees, using a framework representing twigs and branches with flock added. Rubberized horsehair is readily available from model scenery suppliers and makes a good base. However, it is much too dense as supplied, and needs to be teased out to be thinner. It can be supplemented by twisted wires for more substantial bushes or dead wood. Scatter is added, as for a tree. Like trees, they are best made away from the layout and planted later. A few painted cocktail sticks in the ground along the line of the hedge can be used to help secure it.

Garden hedges are usually uniform, while roadside hedges are more varied, with flowering bushes, thin patches, and gaps with bits of fencing.

WALLS

The form of stone walls varies across the country. In areas where stone is uncommon, fences are used. Walls in built-up areas are likely to be much neater and more uniform than field walls.

For field walls there are several suppliers of good-looking cast-resin walls. Osborn's Models produce convincing laser-cut walls that are flexible so can go on uneven ground.

A web search will find a great many different garden and house walls; Farish do dressed stone walls, for example.

For more urban areas stone walls can be made from card covered with stone-effect 'brickpaper'; or use plastic stone sheets, which you then paint.

DAS modelling clay is an air-drying clay, white or brown, which is good for modelling walls. After forming the shape of the wall, scribe gaps between the stones. Paint when the clay is dry. While resin walls are good for long runs that are fairly level, it might be preferable to use DAS for steep sections, or to model a damaged section.

This tree on Wickwar is made from a sprig of Sea foam and still looks good, but the top is rather bare because a lot has broken off as operators have to lean over it to re-rail stock.

A wall made from plastic stone sheet, painted. The tops of such walls consist of large stones mounted vertically; these are modelled using DAS clay. Note the guy wire on the telegraph pole, and the signs done on a computer printer.

FENCES

There are around a hundred different fencing products available in N gauge, ranging from wooden field fencing, through security fencing to garden fencing and ornate gates. They can be moulded plastic, etched metal, and laser cut. Some of the plastic ones are rather heavy in appearance; the etched metal fencing is more delicate. Look for fencing that matches the style you need – for example, the style used by the railway company you are modelling.

A lot of the fencing you will need will be wooden fencing with three bars, though sometimes it will have four or five. Ratio fencing is probably the best of the plastic ones; there are several suppliers of etched fencing. Gates were often metal: N Brass do etched tubular gates.

On level ground just glue the bottoms of the posts into holes made with a small spike. Sloping ground is trickier: the fence posts are always vertical, and on sloping ground the bars are not at right angles to them so need to be bent. Metal fencing can be bent with pliers, bending each rail in turn next to the post. For plastic fencing small notches can be made in the rail next to the post so it is thinner there and easier to bend (the Peco lineside fencing comes like this, though unfortunately it is rather thick). Alternatively use hot water to soften the plastic.

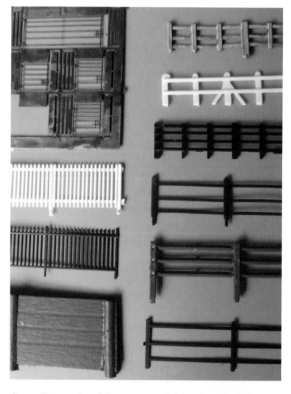

A small sample of fencing available. On the left from the top: N Brass tubular gates (lightly chemically 'blackened'), Ratio GWR station fencing, Ratio spear-point fencing, garden fencing bought on eBay (you can easily do better yourself). On the right: Langley Whitemetal three-bar, Kestrel two-bar, Slater's four-bar, Ratio three-bar, Peco three-bar, Peedie etched three-bar (blackened).

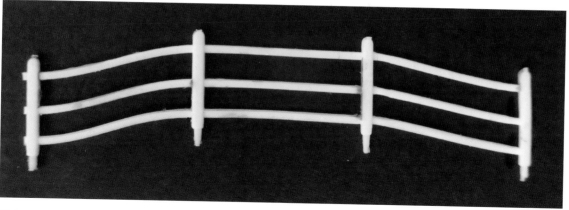

If the posts of plastic fencing are forced into a vertical position the bars form an unnatural-looking S shape, as on the left. Dip them in near boiling water for a few seconds to soften the plastic, then pull to shape and hold while the plastic cools so it looks like the fencing on the right.

For station fencing, for example platform ramps, sloping fencing is usually available to match the level fencing.

Much fencing consists of wood or concrete posts with wire stretched between them. This is easy and cheap to make. For the posts use plastic strip: 0.030in (0.75mm) square is about right. Cut lengths long enough to allow for the part in the ground, and paint them a suitable colour. Cut a strip of card to the height the posts need to be. Cut notches in the edge corresponding to the spacing you want for the posts. Put the first post in place. Then with a notch against that post, drill the next hole where the next

Fencing made from plastic strip posts with E Z Line 'wire' glued on.

notch is. Several can be drilled at a time. If the fence goes up to a baseboard edge the plastic posts are likely to get broken when the boards are erected, so for the end two use metal posts, such as panel pins or 0.8mm nickel-silver wire.

For the wire strands of the fence use rust-coloured E Z Line, 0.25mm thickness. This looks like fine fishing line but it is amazingly elastic – it will stretch to seven times its length without breaking. This elasticity is good for two reasons. By stretching it when you glue it on to the posts it ensures it is tight and straight, but does not put much strain on the posts. Second, if you happen to catch it when working on the layout, rather than breaking or detaching, it just stretches, then returns to its original position.

Attach the lowest wire securely to the end post. I usually wrap it round and glue it. Then with it slightly stretched, glue it to another post, usually several along – although if the ground is uneven you might need to do each post separately. I use a gel superglue. When this is completed, repeat for the other wires. The more wires you have, the harder it is to make the spacing even, so I usually do two.

Concrete posts with the wire can be modelled more accurately if you are prepared to invest the effort. Drill each of the posts with a number of 0.30mm holes for wires, using a jig to ensure they

Ancorton Models and Scale Model Scenery sell kits for security fencing, consisting of mesh and laser-cut posts. The mesh can be mounted either vertically or at 45 degrees, depending on the fence being modelled. The 'barbed wire' is grey cotton.

are uniform. When in position, thread very fine wire through them, perhaps fine guitar wire, which is 0.2mm in diameter, or even finer stainless-steel wire.

Grey thread can be used to represent barbed wire, though plain E Z Line is thinner and closer to scale.

The other style of fencing that is easy to build is modern chain-link security fencing. There are some etched versions available, but I prefer to glue metal mesh to posts. Laser-cut posts can be bought, or made from plastic strip. Paint them concrete colour.

Some fences have the top angled with barbed wire. Suitable mesh is available from a number of suppliers.

Under a fence the grass and weeds are often higher. This can be represented by adding longer static grass in small clumps.

MODELLING WATER

To model water, create the bed as for other scenery, then paint it in suitable colours, typically a dark brown/green colour. Make the colour darker towards the centre to represent deeper water. For shallow water, vegetation can be painted on

A superbly modelled weir on John Birkett-Smith's Totnes layout. Note the careful blending of the scenery into the backscene.

Small river on Wickwar: a painted base with a two-part 'West System Epoxy Resin 105/205' poured over. Small twigs and tiny pebbles have been embedded into the resin. The heron is made from wire, bulked out with solder.

the bottom. Finally add a clear layer over the top: a number of coats of clear varnish can be used, or a single layer of resin or clear drying PVA. There are several companies supplying suitable materials. It is possible to produce ripple effects; the best way depends on the material used, and there are a number of videos on the web. It is easy to make ripples too big: practise away from the layout.

Modelling water that is in violent motion is difficult as it is frozen in time: I would avoid breaking waves and waterfalls. Water that is swirling and has bubbles is rather easier to make look convincing.

The edges of the water are often a problem, as the varnish or resin forms a meniscus, which when scaled up looks completely wrong. One way to avoid it is to add the bank edge after the water, so it covers up the outside few millimetres of 'water' and you can't see the meniscus.

GOING OFF-SCENE

Something that worries a lot of layout builders is how to hide where the track goes into a hole in the backscene. Too often they add a tunnel, but tunnels in many areas are rare and they need to be justi-

The line on Banbury disappears under a road bridge just in front of the backscene.

The line on Wickwar going through the backscene. The tree and a small flap of additional backscene behind the hole help disguise it. We needed additional lighting behind the backscene to illuminate the flap, otherwise it appeared too dark.

fied by the contours of the land. Railway builders avoided them if at all possible.

Any substantial overbridge will hide the track disappearing, particularly if it is in a cutting with a few trees. A steep-sided cutting on its own can work.

In fact you don't need a bridge, the track can just go through a hole. If possible have a tree or building obscuring the exit, but even a plain hole, as there is at one end of Stoney Lane Depot, can work well.

On our Basingstoke layout no attempt was made to hide the edge of the scenic area, and the track simply went into holes in black-painted ply. It sounds terrible, but it was easy to accept that that was the edge of the layout.

BACKSCENES

Creating a good backscene is the biggest improvement you could make to many layouts. It isn't hard: it is easier to paint a tree on a backscene than model one, and even easier if the backscene can be made from photographs.

The higher you can make the backscene the better, particularly for when your layout is photographed. The longer the layout, the higher the backscene needs to be to allow for photographs taken looking along the length. The height is limited by two things. If the layout is operated from behind, it needs to be

low enough for the operator to reach over (I prefer operating from the front to avoid this issue).

Second, if the backscene is part of the baseboards it must be kept low to avoid the baseboards being too bulky for transport. The simple solution to this is to make the backscene a long removable strip that can be rolled up when moving the layout. There are so many advantages to this that I believe almost all portable layouts ought to use a removable backscene:

- You can make it as high as you want without making the baseboards any bigger. The higher the backscene the more 'atmosphere' you create because people are not distracted by what is visible above the backscene.
- The baseboards can be lower: they only need be as high as the highest item of scenery.
- It is continuous, with no gaps in the sky between boards.
- It can be bent round the corners, which is much better than a right-angle in the sky. Even if you have a fixed backscene it will look better with a curved corner.
- You can work on the layout without the backscene restricting access. And the backscene does not get damaged or dirty.
- It is easy to replace if it gets damaged or you decide to improve it.

Erecting the backscene on Wickwar. We have since increased its height by 50 per cent so there is no gap between it and the top canopy, adding to the atmosphere.

There are two disadvantages:

- It is another item to carry, and another job when erecting the layout.
- A fixed backscene provides some protection for the scenery when erecting the layout and working on it, so you may want a low sheet of ply behind where the backscene goes for protection.

The ideal material for a removable backscene is 1mm Foamex board, which is PVC foam sheet. It comes in reasonably priced 8 x 4ft sheets, and most companies that print vinyl banners and signs will have it in stock. It is fairly rigid, but can be rolled to 15in (40cm) diameter. It has a smooth matt white surface that can be painted, or have vinyl printed with a photographic scene attached. Some companies can print on to it directly. Our backscene for Wickwar is 3ft (1m) high and 16ft (5m) long, with self-adhesive vinyl printed with images from photographs, and it cost about £150 including materials, printing, and sticking the vinyl on the Foamex.

We prepared the photographic image ourselves – paying someone to do this would have added a lot to the cost.

The backscene is rolled up and put in a garden waste bin for transport. Roll it with the scene on the inside to avoid damage.

If you need to join lengths of Foamex, fix a 4in (10cm) wide strip of Foamex over the back of the joint with double-sided tape. Do not join it with heavy-duty tape: printers do this for temporary signs, but after being rolled up a few times it stretches and shows up as a line in the printed vinyl.

A problem with any backscene is that it can only look perfect when viewed from one angle. The further away the objects on the backscene, the wider the angle at which it looks acceptable. Objects half a mile or more away will look fine at almost any angle; any closer and distortions will be noticeable. Right-angles on buildings no longer appear to be right-angles; with trees the distortion is less obvious. If you cannot avoid buildings close to on the backscene, arrange that they can only be viewed from a narrow angle – for example looking down a street of buildings.

The colours on the backscene should blend with those colours used for the scenery on the layout immediately in front of it. Using subdued colours for grass on the scenery and bright green on the backscene looks odd and artificial.

If you are painting the backscene you can make the colours match the scenery; if it is printed you have less control, and the scenery must match the backscene. The grass colour can be adjusted by

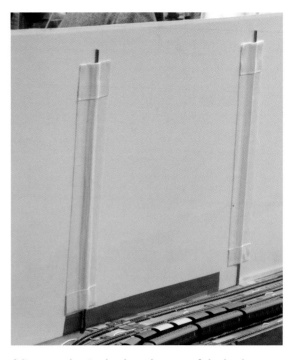

A linen pocket is glued on the rear of the backscene every 12in (30cm), into which a 4mm-diameter stainless-steel rod is inserted, which then goes into a brass tube set into the baseboard. Beading glued to the top of the baseboard between each pair of brass tubes forms a channel into which the bottom of the backscene fits.

The London river view on Lighterman's Yard. The buildings on the backscene are on the far side of the Thames, and the distance reduces distortion.

adding a little more static grass of a different colour, or even weathering it with an airbrush. If possible make the backscene before you do the scenery, and do the blending under the layout lighting.

Continue any feature in the front of the back-scene on to the layout where possible: a hedge, a path, or a group of trees on the backscene augmented by one or two similar trees on the layout. It helps blend it in and disguise the join.

PAINTING BACKSCENES

Sometimes a backscene that is just plain sky can be very effective, and it is certainly easy. It can work well if the land being depicted is as high or higher than most of the land behind. A substantial hedge or wall just in front of the backscene hides the join and will look good viewed from a low angle, and most photos will be taken from low down.

Plain sky can also work well if there is a solid row of buildings in front of it. Any attempt to show the roofs of buildings behind will look odd from most angles.

An amazing sky would distract attention from the layout, so aim for a fairly ordinary sky. Start with white and light blue paint, possibly a little grey, and paint the whole backscene with them, making the sky whiter towards the horizon. Don't use too deep a blue or it can overwhelm the colours on the layout. Then add clouds using white. An airbrush is ideal, but I have managed good effects using cans of Halford's white primer. Just white is fine for wispy clouds, but for heavier-looking clouds you need to add some grey as well.

Look at a few clouds on a suitable day – take pictures and note the colours. Start with the white, and spray it moving along with a circular motion so you get an uneven upper edge to the cloud. Fill in below to make the cloud as deep as you want, holding the airbrush or can further away when doing the bottom so it is wispier. If you want to add in shadows in the lower parts with the grey, only use small amounts. If using a spraycan it may be best to add a little and then spread it with a paintbrush, or use a ball of sponge on the end of a stick. Don't have too much contrast between clouds and sky colour – it makes them stand out more, and you want them not to be noticed.

Distant hills are easy to paint on the bottom of your sky: I use artist's acrylic paints. You need just a few colours, and to mix them: white is important. The further away the hills are, the paler they will appear, and their colour will become bluer. Very distant mountains can appear a purple/grey. The main thing to remember is that they should never be brighter or more vivid than the colours in front of them on the layout.

Painted backscene on Bolden. It is a plain sky with a few close-up trees and distant hills. Flock has been added to the painted trees to give them a 3D appearance.

CREATING A PHOTOGRAPHIC BACKSCENE

It is important to have a good photo-editing package: Photoshop is the market leader, and an old version will suffice. GIMP is an open source alternative. I didn't know anything about Photoshop when I started on Wickwar's backscene, but I learned as I went, though it would have been faster if I had watched some online guides first and read the manual!

You need photographs, and you need them taken in appropriate light, so choose a day that has the right conditions. Bright sunlight creates a lot of shadows – a bright but overcast day is better. What photos you need depends on the topography. If everything on the backscene will be hills a mile or more away, a panoramic shot from a suitable viewpoint will probably suffice (most modern cameras can take these).

Wickwar is in a narrow valley, and the horizon is only about 400 yards away. We found that shots taken straight on to where the backscene would be were fine, but the more you panned sideways, the more the image you needed was compressed, resulting in the completed image being too short. We took a series of shots as we walked along the opposite side of the valley, with the camera pointing directly at the 'backscene'. Clouds change between shots so you will end up 'drawing' most of them in Photoshop by copying clouds from other photos.

Only 300DPI is needed for printing vinyl, and 150DPI is almost as good. While there is software that will join multiple photos to make a panorama, none that I tried did a good enough job so I did it manually, one photo at a time, starting with the photo in the centre. Photos were added alongside, cropping them as was necessary. Often the colours needed adjusting to compensate for different lighting. A few needed resizing to match the adjacent photo, or rotating by a small angle. Sometimes the photos joined well, but usually I had to use the clone stamp tool to touch up the join. This copies a small circular area from one part of the picture to another: more is copied by moving the cursor around like a brush. I did all this work zoomed in a long way: if it looks acceptable like this, it will be fine viewed normally.

There will be areas you need to 'paint out' of the image – for example, a building in front of the backscene that is modelled on the layout, or a modern structure that has to be removed. We were lucky that the view at Wickwar had hardly changed in sixty years. I used the same clone stamp tool to remove unwanted features, or I copied an area from another photo and added it in.

One of the photos used for the backscene on Wickwar. This photo required more editing than any other. The brewery and trees in the foreground had to be painted out. The photo was taken at an angle so it was too short, so a slice had to be duplicated and inserted to make the field wider. The sky had to be extended upwards.

The area of the completed backscene, extended by duplicating a slice.

Usually the photos needed stretching to conform with the model, and simply scaling up the whole could make the horizon too high; in fact having it at the correct scale height looked wrong on Wickwar, probably because it is usually viewed from slightly above. I found you could stretch by about 15 per cent without trees looking odd, but not much more. Where this was insufficient, I duplicated a slice of the photo to increase the length. Provided you take an area without many distinguishing features,

this works well. Edit any distinctive items, such as a strangely shaped tree, so the duplication is not obvious. I repeatedly printed out A4 sections of the image, taped them together, and tried them out against the layout to see how it looked.

The sky was largely copied from other photos. For the left-hand side I went for plain blue sky, using the gradient tool: this lets you pick a rectangular area with colour on two opposite edges, and fills it with smoothly changing colour.

CHAPTER SEVEN

BUILDINGS AND SIGNALS

BUILDINGS

It is possible to buy many buildings, both complete and kits, but a much wider range of buildings will be needed to achieve a high level of authenticity. You may be lucky and find station buildings for the railway company you are modelling or houses in the style of the area modelled, but more often you will need to scratch-build or heavily adapt kits to get the buildings you want. Don't be tempted to use a building in the wrong style just because it is available and looks pretty, because it will not look right on the completed model.

It is possible to mix buildings in different materials, but care is needed to make them match. For example, if you have brick buildings finished with both painted plastic and brickpaper, the plastic building needs to be well weathered if it is to match the brickpaper, rather than being a uniform brick colour.

A number of companies make resin-moulded buildings, often available both painted and unpainted. One of the largest and best ranges is Farish Scenecraft. There is little scope for modifying them, and some of the more basic models have solid windows.

Plastic kits assemble into well-detailed models. It is possible to modify and vary how you build them. The range is limited: Ratio has line-side buildings including stations and signal boxes, Kestrel has a more extensive range, Faller has a vast range of continental buildings, Japanese companies have interesting industrial buildings.

A few etched metal kits are available, many from a fairly new supplier, Severn Models, whose range includes cottages, small buildings, details such as garden frames, pit-head winding-gear kit, and an electricity pylon. The detail is very fine and they look convincing. They can be assembled with superglue rather than solder.

Claydon makes good use of ready-painted resin buildings from the SD Mouldings range.

Kestrel plastic kits of a church, houses and bungalow on our club layout Bolden. The bridge is from Peco.

The signal box on Wickwar is an etched brass kit for a Midland box by Churchward Models. Because Midland boxes were built from prefabricated panels, it was easy to adapt the four-panel kit to the three-wide Wickwar box. The interior is a Ratio kit.

MAKE YOUR BUILDINGS EASY TO REMOVE

If (when) damage occurs, such as when a window gets pushed in, it is easier to work on the building away from the layout. If at a later stage you decide to add lighting or improve the interior you will need to remove the building. And if you have fitted lights you want to be able to get at them if they fail. If you do fix the building down, only use a small dab of glue in each corner, or use magnets.

Photos will show up any gap between the bottom of a building's wall and the ground – these are commonly referred to as 'floating buildings'. To avoid gaps, put the building in a recess so the walls go below ground level. The recess can be very shallow, just strips of cardboard round the outside. It might be the pavement. Buildings I make myself have an extra centimetre or more on the bottom, which is buried in the ground. When using foam as the base of the scenery, making a hole is easy, and if it is a tight fit it will hold the building without any glue. If a building has a visible gap, add static grass to hide it.

The hotel on Wickwar pulled out of its hole. This can be done without damaging the scenery. It allows access to wiring for lighting, and to the speaker that is concealed inside for sound effects.

CARD BUILDINGS

It is likely most of the buildings on your layout will be of card: it is cheap and flexible, and there are plenty of suppliers of both kits and brickpaper.

There are lots of kits of varying difficulty, or you can start from a drawing and make everything from card and brickpaper. If you begin by making a few card kits it will give you the confidence and skills to move on to scratch-building.

Several manufacturers produce kits of pre-printed and cut card. They come with detailed instructions, also with additional components needed for finishing, perhaps printed windows or chimney pots. They are easy to build, and go together rapidly. Details such as drainpipes may need to be added.

All buildings made of card will have a few white edges that need painting to hide them. The easy way is to use paint pencils, which have a centre of watercolour paint. They come in a wide range of colours, and all art shops stock them. To use, dampen the tip and run it along the edge.

There are often several related kits that can be joined together in different ways. As you gain experience you will be able to modify them and join them

Metcalfe card kits have pre-cut card parts and include glazing; they can be assembled rapidly. Similar are Prototype Models' kits, which often include plastic parts.

My collection of paint pencils. For buildings I mainly use the two darker greys and the dark red-brown; they look lighter when applied, so buy dark colours. The orange and white on the left are more for weathering – for example, fresh rust or chalk marks on wagons.

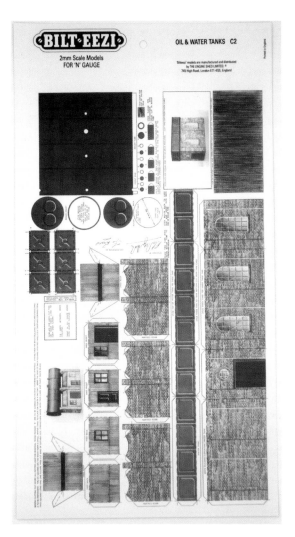

Bilteezi kits are a simple sheet of card that can still build into a satisfying model, particularly if you add details.

in ways not in the instructions to produce a building that suits the space you have.

The most basic kits are the Bilteezi range from Freestone Models: these are just printed card sheets that you cut out, then cardboard can be added as needed.

A huge number of card building kits are available to download from the web for a modest fee. These come in the form of a PDF document with a number of coloured pages to print on an inkjet printer, and another that has the instructions. Many sites offer one or two free kits of small buildings to try out. Seal the printed sheets with acrylic spray varnish, otherwise the colours will run when glued. You can print it as many times as you want; even if you only want one you can reprint a sheet if you make a mistake. The pages need to be stuck on to card and then cut out. The main work is cutting out all the parts, but apart from that they are not very different to a pre-cut card kit.

Use matt-coated inkjet paper, as thin as you can find. I usually use 120gsm paper, though it is possible to find 100gsm paper.

The quality of the downloaded kits varies, sometimes in the quality of the images, but more often in the number of different parts and the complexity of the design. One semi-detached might be little more than a box, and another will have bay windows, a recessed porch and a conservatory. The more complex one is not necessarily better: if all you need is a box in a distant corner of the layout, the simpler one may be better.

Scalescenes has an extensive range of buildings. They are top quality with detailed instructions.

A castle/folly built from a Scalescenes kit. The only parts not in the kit are the railings (an etch) and the flagpole.

They take longer to build than others, but the results justify the extra time it takes. You might want to omit some details: for example, there are often components to make a highly detailed interior, but unless you install lighting you won't see it. A problem I have had with the N-gauge Scalescenes kits is that when you have to glue several layers of card into a block, as when making a chimney stack, the block is often slightly too thick for the paper to be wrapped round it. Check before gluing, and make one of the layers of card thinner if necessary.

These kits are designed so everything can be built from card, but sometimes using plastic strip or an etched detail would be better. For example, thin strips of card are not the ideal material for railings – using plastic railings or making them out of plastic strip is faster and would give a better result.

TURNING PHOTOS INTO MODELS

If you have photographs of a building you want to model, why not turn them into something like a downloaded kit? This will give an accurate model of the building with the correct brick or stone, and ready weathered. Details such as arches and decorative stonework are already in place, so there is no need to mark everything out.

The hotel on Wickwar is from photos. This is one of several pictures I used.

The first requirement is to take photographs of all the sides in good light with no strong shadows – a bright but overcast day is ideal. March can be a good time, with few leaves on the trees but often good light. Photographs should be taken as close to square-on as you can manage, and from as far away as possible to minimize distortion. Obstructions such as people, cars, trees, bushes or telephone boxes between the camera and the building should be avoided. Sometimes this is possible, others will just have to be photo-edited out.

If your photos are not ideal, more time will have to be spent editing. Take down the basic dimensions so you can scale the photographs: the total height, length and depth of the building.

You need photo-editing software. You can teach yourself to use it, as I have done: there is nothing complicated to do. The package must be able to 'distort' the image so that lines that should be vertical or horizontal are represented correctly. I use Photoshop, and the instructions below relate to it, but most of these packages work in a similar way.

To make your photo right for the model the steps are as follows:

Step 1: Create a copy of the background layer using 'Layer/Duplicate Layer', then use the 'Edit/ Transform/Distort' command to make the top and bottom of the building horizontal and the sides vertical. Use 'View/Show/Grid' to display grid lines over the image so you can judge when it is exactly square.

Step 2: Crop the photo to just the area you need. You may want to leave a little extra on the bottom if you plan to make the building fit into a shallow hole in the ground to avoid gaps under the walls.

Step 3: Work out the size you want the printed image to be, from the height and width of the actual building. Use the 'Resize Image' command to change the size to be correct. You must uncheck the 'constrain proportions' box in order to change the ratio between horizontal and vertical dimensions. Set the resolution to the number of pixels per inch you intend to print, otherwise you may lose detail. I suggest selecting 600 pixels per inch.

Larger buildings, particularly industrial ones, often have panels that repeat along the building. Once you have created one panel, you can print it as many times as needed. You may want to make an image wider. With the protruding buttresses on Wickwar Brewery I had to extend the edges so as to provide something to wrap round the sides. You may need to adjust brightness, contrast and colours to make the different sides match.

Finally unwanted items have to be edited out, and the image extended to fill in hidden areas. There are two main ways to do this. First, put a rectangle round the part of the picture you want to copy ('Marquee' tool), key 'CTRL-C' to copy it, select the move tool, and key 'CTRL-V' to create a copy of the area in a new layer. You can then move it around to position it over the part you want to cover up.

For smaller details use the 'Clone Stamp' tool, represented by a rubber stamp icon. First select a 'brush' of the size you want – for copying bricks choose one a little smaller than their height. Click

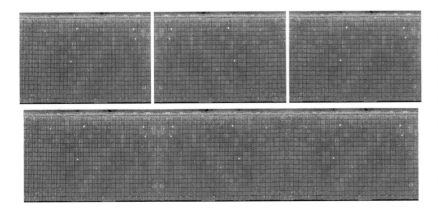

Extending a small area of roof tiles to be wider. At the top left is the original, and on the right is a straight copy. In the centre is another copy, but flipped horizontally, so left becomes right. As the edges next to each other are identical, when joined together at the bottom they match well.

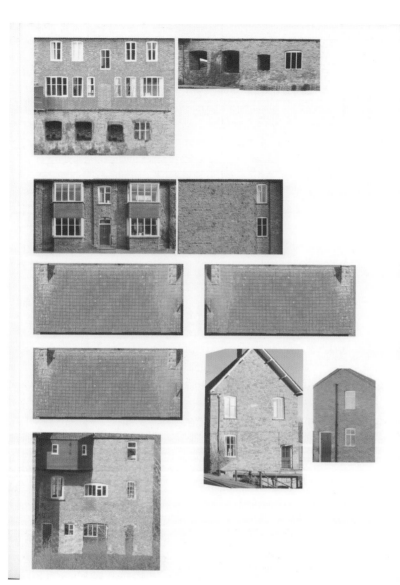

After editing all the photos I had this 'kit' ready to be printed. It is very similar to a downloaded card kit.

forms a sharper edge when you copy. It is possible to copy from a different image as well as from the image being worked on. Save your results at regular intervals to differently named copies of the image so you can go back if needed, though most of the time the CTRL-Z key ('undo last action') is all you need if you make a mistake. You need to use 'Merge Layers' regularly to get rid of additional layers created.

Print using an inkjet printer on to matt photo paper. Experiment with different paper and print quality settings to see which gives the best results: photo quality is not always best. After printing, spray the sheet with an acrylic matt varnish to protect the ink from running if it gets wet when gluing it.

on the part of the image you want to copy from, with the 'Alt' key held down. Then move the brush to where you want the copy to go. Click and keep your finger down, so the button is not released, then as you move the cursor around it copies from the original location to under the brush.

This is easier to understand in practice than from a written description. You can practise as many times as you like provided you don't save the results. You can choose several types of brush; a harder one

Once you have the images for the building, it can be constructed just as a downloaded kit for a building would be. Most parts will need to be stuck on to card. You might want to cut out windows and doors to improve their appearance with relief or glazing.

A good model of a building can be achieved with surprisingly little work. In less than an hour I made a mock-up of the hotel that looked fine from any distance, by sticking photos on a block of polystyrene.

The completed hotel installed on Wickwar. The 'kit' was built by another member of the team.

SCRATCH-BUILDING MATERIALS

If modelling a real location, many of the buildings will have to be made from scratch. Even if you are not modelling a real location, look for unusual buildings that will look good on your layout – it will be more interesting as a result.

Building papers, often referred to as brickpaper, are sheets of paper coloured to represent bricks, stonework, roofing and paving. They can be bought ready printed: Freestone Models has a wide range, for example. Many more are available for download: you pay a small fee and print them yourself. You can print as many copies as you want. You should be able to find a good match for what you need, and if it is not quite right you can scale it when printing, or adjust the colours in a photo-editing package. (You may need to convert the download to be editable – there are free web sites that will do this.) Print on thin, matt-coated inkjet paper, and apply two coats of matt or satin acrylic spray varnish before using, to seal the colours and protect from fading.

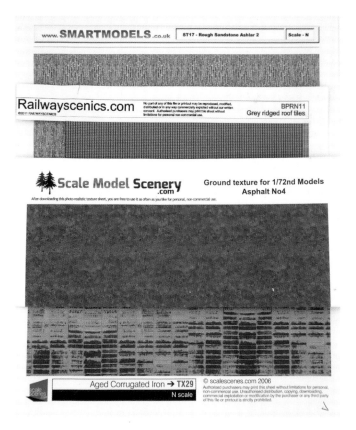

A selection of brickpapers I have used. From the top: Smartmodels rough sandstone ashlar, Railway Scenics grey ridged roof tiles (colour adjusted), Scale Model Scenery asphalt, and Scalescenes rusted corrugated iron.

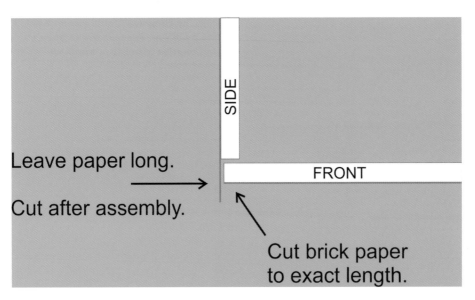

SIDE

FRONT

Leave paper long.

Cut after assembly.

Cut brick paper to exact length.

At corners leave extra paper beyond the end of the side to cover the end of the front or rear. After assembly cut off any excess, and colour the exposed white edge with a paint pencil.

If possible stick the paper to the sides of the building before assembly. I recommend using a glue stick. Apply it fairly thickly, then press the paper on with a small roller of the type used by decorators.

Redutex is a Spanish firm that makes a range of flexible embossed sheets with a self-adhesive backing. They include stonework, brickwork, corrugated roofs and paving. The corrugated roofing in particular is excellent, and the pantiles and slate roofs are also very good.

Cut a piece the size you want and stick it on to card. It is quite thick, so when using Redutex roofing, have the edge that overhangs beyond the walls with no card backing, otherwise it will look too thick. It is expensive, but you don't need much in N gauge. DCC Supplies distributes it in the UK.

An alternative to paper is to use an embossed plastic sheet and paint it. For N gauge I don't use this for brick-work as the relief is over-scale: mortar is more or less level with the bricks. Further, a printed sheet is already

Selection of different Redutex sheets. Many come in both plain and weathered versions, such as the corrugated grey roofing shown.

The roofs on the two buildings in the foreground are of Redutex, as are the roof and side of the polygonal building, and some of the roofs further away.

A scalpel blade can be resharpened many times with an oilstone: it takes no more time than changing the blade, and costs nothing. Also shown is my favourite ruler for cutting card. It is clear plastic with a 1cm grid marked so it is easy to line up, and it has a metal strip along the far edge so can be used with a scalpel without damaging it.

coloured with variation between different bricks. Embossed sheets can look good for stonework, but to get the best out of them you need to spend a lot of time picking out individual stones in slightly different colours and weathering.

Embossed sheets with grooves are good for wood, planking and clapboard. Evergreen has a range of different spacings and groove types. The wooden house illustrated later uses this sheeting.

While it is possible to make models from old Cornflakes packets, I like to buy good quality card as it is easier to work with. I use artist's mountboard, available from art shops or online. It has a uniform dense texture that makes it easy to cut and shape. It often comes with one black and one white side, which can be convenient. It is 1.4mm thick, ideal for the sides of buildings. For smaller details I use thick white card.

When cutting card, particularly thicker card such as mountboard, you need a very sharp blade in your scalpel or craft knife. Cutting cardboard soon blunts a knife, but they sharpen well on an oilstone.

Don't try to cut all the way through in one go – make a number of lighter cuts. The harder you press

down, the more the blade is likely to wander off the straight. Use a metal-edged ruler for cutting, placed over the part you want to keep so if the blade does stray it is into the scrap area. For short cuts, the length of the blade or less, dispense with the ruler and cut by eye, aided if needed by magnification. If you use a curved blade you can rock it to deepen the cut.

To get an exact fit, parts can be filed to size using an emery-board nail file.

A finishing layer will usually need to be added on top. Concrete can be painted with matt paint. For pebbledash, talcum powder might be sprinkled on top of the paint.

I have a stock of plastic sheet and strip in various thicknesses, mainly used for adding details. I use a lot of plastic strip – it is simple and gives a neat appearance, as the sides are always perfectly straight.

When cutting plastic do not cut all the way through. It is faster and gives a neater line if you only cut or score about half way, then bend it. It will snap off along the half-cut line.

MAKING A BUILDING FROM SCRATCH

Get photographs of the building you want to model, or a building in the style you want to model. Draw up rough plans of the building with all the key dimensions so you can plan how it will fit together, and so it matches the space you have – you may have to compress some parts.

From this, work out the sizes of the thick card pieces that will form the carcase of the building,

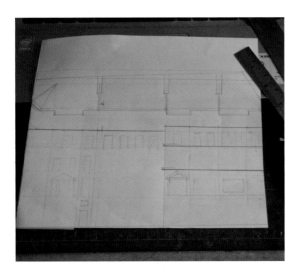

The initial rough drawing for one of Grahame Hedges' excellent buildings.

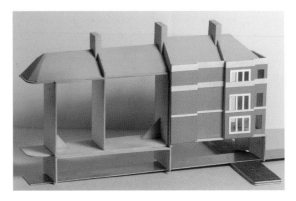

Carcase of the building made from mountboard, with cladding added on the right.

draw them on mountboard, and cut them out. Mark and cut out any windows, doors, and so on. Cover with brickpaper or cladding, and assemble the building, then add details.

It is not as hard to do as most people think!

WINDOWS

The simplest representation is printed paper, with the 'glass' dark. Though it sounds crude, it can look very effective, particularly away from the front of the layout. Putting a sheet of clear plastic over the top can improve the appearance.

You can print your own windows from a photo taken square on. When taking the photo, be careful of lighting and reflections: you want to avoid the glass catching the light – it is better if it looks dark.

If the interior is to be visible you need clear windows. It is difficult to see into domestic buildings in N unless they are right at the front of the layout or illuminated. Large windows in shops and offices are easier to look through and need to be clear.

The two buildings shown have large windows. Sheets of clear plastic are readily available from model shops and the internet. There are two main types: styrene sheet and acetate sheet. Styrene can be glued with standard plastic glues, but is more easily scratched and fogged by glues; on the whole I prefer acetate.

A danger with clear windows is that it is possible to see things you shouldn't be able to see. You don't

The finished building, with windows, glazing and guttering added, then painted and weathered.

The brewery office on Wickwar has printed windows from a photograph. The upper windows show a shadowy image of the interior and reflect the trees opposite; this looks more realistic than a clear glazed window would. Most windows look better if a hole is cut in the building side and the printed window mounted on the back, so you get the relief at the sides of the window opening.

want to be able to look in at an upper front window and out of one on the ground floor. You need floors and walls to block the view, though these can be very basic.

Some kits come with windows printed on clear plastic, and they may be available separately, or you may have some left over from kits you have bought. Scalescenes has a range called Scaleglaze that is sold separately. Freestone Models sells sheets, Scene-Setters, with white glazing bars printed in a regular grid that can be used for different-sized windows.

Printed windows are typically only available in white, but nearly all window frames are white. It is possible to draw directly on to a clear plastic with a bow pen or a paint pen. Draw the window scale-size on paper first. An easy way is to create an empty table in Word, with cells the correct size for the panes, and print it. Put the paper under the acetate, then trace over the lines.

The final method is to have separate frames with clear glazing stuck behind. The frames can be painted first, in any colour you like. They provide relief between frame and glass, so look better

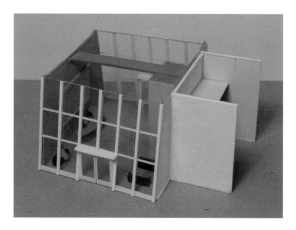

The interior of this atrium will be visible in normal lighting, so an interior is needed.

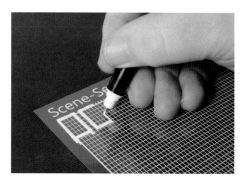

Scene-Setters glazing. Cut out a rectangle with the number of panes needed, plus an overlap round each edge, and thicken up the edges for the outside frame using a paint pen on the outside of the lines. The printed lines are slightly raised so act as a guide.

The bottling plant has interior lighting, so the representation of a conveyor belt for packing bottles can be seen.

viewed close up. For windows with complex curved patterns, such as church windows, they are almost essential. There are suppliers producing frames in moulded plastic, laser-cut plastic sheet, and etched brass.

If a standard sash window or a GWR station window is needed there may be a choice of suppliers – though often you will have to compromise. However, you can make your own windows.

A simple (if fiddly) way is to take a printed window, for example from a photo, and carefully cut out each

frame of glass. A variant on this method is to print the window on to a self-adhesive label and cut the panes out.

Another technique is using self-adhesive address labels cut into thin strips with a scalpel. Try to only cut through the paper, not the backing sheet. Lay strips on to clear plastic to form the windows. Do the horizontal bars first, and then the vertical. Again, it helps to draw the window on paper first, and put this under the clear plastic as a guide. Don't worry if the strips you cut are not all uniform width – just use the best ones. Bars that are not quite square can be pushed to a better position with the end of a scalpel blade. The method is best for white frames, though it is possible to colour the frames with water paint.

You can buy plastic sheets with patterns printed on them. York Model Rail has several sheets of 'stained glass', and Scene Setters from Freestone Models has sheets printed with a grey grid to represent leaded glass (though the spacing is a little large for N). Scale Model Scenery does a sheet with protective blast tape, as used during World War II.

The clearest glazing of all is glass. It can be bought in thin sheets as microscope cover slides in various sizes. Wickwar signal box shown earlier in this chapter has cover-slide glazing behind etched frames to allow a good view of the interior.

The brewery windows left and centre are printed photographs with the 'glass' cut out leaving the glazing bars, with clear plastic behind. The windows on the right are simply printed on paper.

To cut out windows, make two short cuts into the corner of each pane, eight cuts per pane. Use a very sharp blade, and magnification such as an Optivisor.

To attach the glazing I use a gel superglue. Some people recommend using an impact adhesive such as UHU or Bostik Clear to avoid any danger of fogging the windows, but I have not had this problem. Other people prefer a clear-drying PVA-based glue. Whatever glue you use, the important thing is to use it very sparingly and keep it away from the visible parts of the glazing. A small dot in each outside corner will usually be sufficient: it doesn't need a lot of strength.

Hold the window glazing (with bars) in tweezers and manoeuvre it into position while looking at the front of the building to ensure accurate placement – do not 'slide' it into position because you will get glue on the glazing in the visible area.

Wooden house on Wickwar. The windows are acetate with strips of label attached as glazing bars. The window frames and guttering are plastic strip, and the house sides are plastic sheeting.

Microscope cover slides. To cut them, put them on a hard, flat surface (not a cutting mat) and score them lightly with a tungsten carbide-tipped cutter, then snap along the scored line. Do not use a wheel cutter, as it will crack the glass.

DETAILING AND CUSTOMISING

Plastic strip or wire can be used for details such as capping stones and drainpipes. Television aerials can be soldered from wire. For chimney pots, some of the insulation from the live (brown) wire on mains cable works better than a rolled-up paper tube. Thin lead foil from a wine bottle can be used for flashing — it covers up unsightly gaps at the same time. Half-round plastic strip makes excellent guttering.

Many companies sell a few parts that can be used to detail models, but it can be difficult to find specific items. Ask on a forum or email group devoted to N gauge if you fail to find what you want. The following are just a few manufacturers and the products they provide:

Fretcetera (Scalelinkfretcetera.co.uk): Etched components, many different styles of gates and fencing, windows, iron staircases, clock faces and ornate brackets (the range used to be marketed by Scalelink).

York Modelmaking (yorkmodelrail.com): Laser-cut details including windows, valences, doors.

Gold Medal Models (goldmm.com): Etches to 1:160 including television aerials, fire escapes and Venetian blinds.

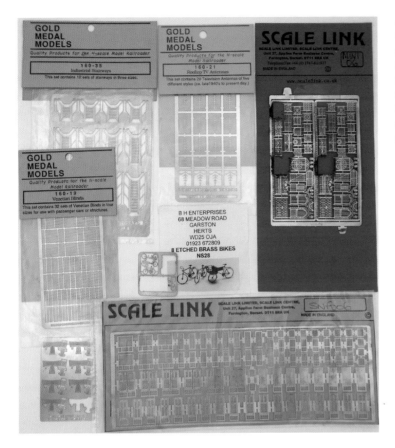

A selection of etches. Some of the Gold Medal etches are stainless steel, which is thinner and finer than brass and nickel silver, such as the etch at bottom left for a shopping trolley. The gates removed from the Scalelink fret had been chemically blackened, which is more easily done while they are still on the fret.

B.H. Enterprises: Sells a vast range of N-gauge kits and detailing items.

Much of the time viewers will be looking down on the layout, so roofs are very important, and it is worth spending time on chimneys, television aerials and loft conversions.

SIGNALS

To work out where signals are needed, look at signalling diagrams for similar locations. There are plenty available on the web and in books.

People notice signals changing when they are standing on a platform, so it is good to make them work on your model. But even on small layouts, operators often don't have time to operate signals, so I like to automate them using train detection. For example, change the signal to clear when a train passes a point some distance before the signal, and put it back to danger after the loco has passed the signal. It may not be prototypically correct, but it is close, and then trains won't be going past signals at danger.

Ratio makes a range of semaphore signal kits. Their kit for remote control only provides manual remote operation by a length of thread. I prefer to operate the signals using a servo below the board, connected by 0.3mm NS wire. You don't need the remote-control kit. The arm and pivot are quite delicate, and to protect them the movement of the wire should be limited, as described later.

The only ready-made working semaphore signals are from Dapol. Power them from a 9–12V-regulated

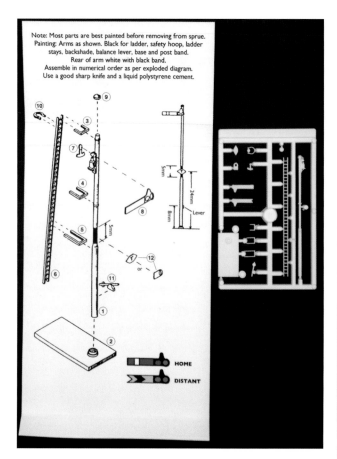

Note: Most parts are best painted before removing from sprue. Painting: Arms as shown. Black for ladder, safety hoop, ladder stays, backshade, balance lever, base and post band. Rear of arm white with black band. Assemble in numerical order as per exploded diagram. Use a good sharp knife and a liquid polystyrene cement.

The Ratio signal kit builds into a very accurate model. An etched ladder and safety hoops are available separately for an even finer appearance.

DC supply – an old phone charger is ideal if it is a suitable voltage; the earlier instructions said to use 15V AC, but this could burn out the motor. The electrics don't let you set a specific aspect – you can only tell it to change to the opposite of what it is showing. So you have to check its position each time, and if you have automated operation when you turn the layout on, you have to tell it what position the signal is currently in. A kit is available from MERG to upgrade it to have positive setting of the aspect.

I prefer to make my own semaphore signals, partly because you can make them closer to scale and more delicate in appearance, and partly for the robustness of all-metal construction, but mainly because many signals are not standard. On Wickwar

Dapol signals look good, though not as fine in appearance as the Ratio ones. Replacing the signal arm with a metal one would be an improvement.

there are three semaphore signals. The two north of the station are very tall to improve visibility; the one by the signal box is on a bracket over the track so it is visible round the curve to the tunnel. Signals on station platforms are often shorter than usual.

The signal arms are from Model Signal Engineering. The posts are brass tube from Eileen's Emporium, 1mm OD tube or rod for the upper part, with 1.2mm OD/1mm ID tube for the thicker lower part. This is close to scale for LMS and GWR signal posts.

Model Signal Engineering (MSE) provides a comprehensive range of components from which to construct your own signals. These include signal arms (of many types), ladders, posts (including lattice posts), and some components for bracket signals.

The Wickwar signals are removable for ease of maintenance, and those in exposed positions are removed when the layout is taken down. A strip of tinplate glued to the signal base holds it against a magnet glued to the baseboard.

If you operate your layout in a night mode you need lights, and you want them anyway. Use a warm white SMD LED, glued to the post behind the arm. Power it using the metal post and metal ladder as

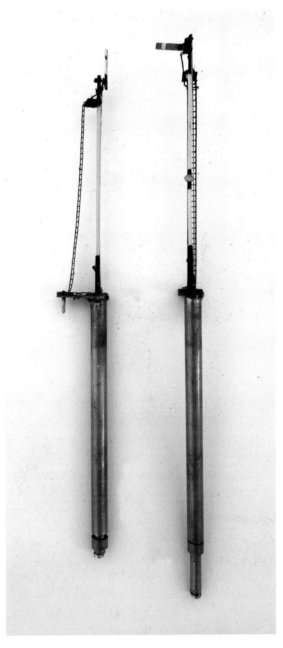

The signal base is a rectangle of double-sided PCB, to which the signal post is soldered. The ladder goes up to a platform, another piece of PCB, and is soldered at both ends. Soldered under the base below the post is a length of (larger) tube that fits within a tube recessed into the baseboard. At the front of the base, under the end of the ladder, is a pin going into thin tube in the baseboard, partly to ensure the signal faces in the right direction, but mainly as a second electrical connection for a light.

the two 'wires'. The copper on the PCB for both base and platform must be gapped to avoid a short. MSE sells film in different colours: small pieces glued to the rear of the spectacle on the arm show as green, red or amber when illuminated by an LED behind.

All signals have railings round the platform. These can be made out of soldered wire.

If you want to operate signals made from Model Signal Engineering parts you have to pivot the arm. Solder a pin of 0.3mm nickel-silver wire to the rear of the arm at right angles, and put it in a 2mm length of brass tube soldered to the side of the post. Keep the arm in place with a ring of the insulation from thin wire pushed on the end of the pin.

To operate simple post signals, use 0.3mm nickel-silver wire attached to the end of the arm. This goes through a brass guide tube at the base of the signal to a servo motor under the layout. Because the arm and its pivot are delicate, add stops of short lengths of brass tube, soldered to the operating wire each side of the tube at the base to restrict its movement. It means you don't have to worry about fine adjustment of the servo – just bend a loop in the wire from the servo to take up excess movement. The stops can be adjusted if necessary by touching a soldering iron to them and pushing them along the wire.

As the signal is removable it cannot be permanently connected to the servo. The signal wire is connected to a brass tube with a 3mm magnet glued on the end. This tube slides inside the tube below the base. Another magnet is attached to the end of the wire from the servo. When the signal is inserted through the baseboard the two magnets couple up to each other automatically.

Life is easier if you use colour light signals, as there are several manufacturers of working signals, for example Berko and Heathcote Electronics. We have become used to steady improvements in the quality of products in N gauge, though unusually the situation was better some years ago when the Roger Murray range of custom-build signals was available –

This bracket signal is built in a similar way. It uses a stiff operating wire, bent through a right-angle at the base of the signal dolly (the short post on which the arm is mounted) and at the top of the main post.

then you could get working 'feathers' (the row of white lights that indicate a diverging route is set) and calling on lights, something you would have to scratch-build now.

The N Brass range of kits for various colour light signals is designed to have lights fitted, and would be a good starting point for making more complex signals.

There are many markings, boards and additional indications found on signal posts. Modern signals all have a signal number on a board on the post. A white diamond is often seen. This indicates that the line is track circuited, so it is not necessary to send the fireman to the signal box under rule 55. Sometimes to aid visibility a white board was mounted behind a semaphore arm; this was common if the signal was in front of a bridge.

Ground signals were used to control shunting and loco movements around stations. These were small white discs with a red or occasionally yellow bar across, or more recently colour light signals of

A working colour light signal built from an N Brass kit.

A two-aspect colour light signal, from the huge range produced by Berko.

triangular form. N Brass offers kits for both types. It isn't difficult to make working colour-light ground signals, and I know one person who has produced a working disc signal. However, it is doubtful you would actually operate them, or that anyone would notice if you did.

A ground signal. The post is a strip of PCB, but plastic could be used. It fits in a rectangular brass tube set into the baseboard, so it can be removed when cleaning the track. To make the disc, I painted a red stripe across a sheet of thin white plasticard and then cut out the disc with a hole punch, the type used for making holes in belts. The 2.5mm hole is the right size. The difficult part is getting the stripe dead centre. This is much easier if you punch it out after painting the stripe. When putting them on the layout check that none of your larger locos will hit them (the Dapol 9F and new Farish 8F are the widest I have).

CHAPTER EIGHT

ROLLING STOCK

KIT BUILDING

If you are modelling post World War II, most of the stock you need will be available. For Wickwar, we built a Patriot loco from a kit and a few LMS coaches: two ordinary coaches (one earlier than available and one later), a buffet car, a kitchen car and three TPO coaches. We built more wagons, though mainly to add variety and because kit building is enjoyable. Only one important type was not available 'ready to run' (RTR): an LMS/BR banana van.

GOODS WAGONS

A wide range of wagon kits is available, including many from the N-Gauge Society. Most are easy to build, a body fitting on an RTR chassis or bogies, and most liveries are simple to paint. Non-passenger coaching stock kits such as parcels vans are equally simple. If you need a lot of a particular wagon, kits work out much cheaper than RTR, and allow you to add variety with different details, markings and weathering.

As well as assembling them as intended, kits can be modified to represent variations or similar

The NGS SR van kit includes even planking, uneven planking, and ply sides, representing the three basic types built. To replace a planked door with a ply one, use a razor saw to remove the door from a ply side, sawing just outside the edges of the door (left). File to the exact edge of the door: lay a large file flat on the bench and rub the side over it. Then do the same on a planked side (right), this time cutting just inside the door and filing the sides down to the exact size. Place the three parts together and check they fit squarely and without gaps, and that the total length is exactly the same as an original side. If not, file a little more.

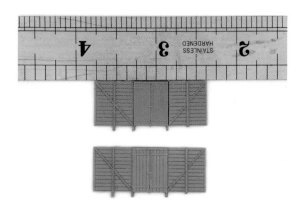

When happy that the pieces fit together squarely and are the same length as the original side (below), glue them together face up on a flat surface so the back is flat, pushing the top edge against a ruler to ensure it is perfectly straight. To get a strong bond, slide the parts up and down against each other before the glue sets. Leave to dry, then assemble as normal.

Three modified vans. On the left, diagonal strapping made from foil has been added to an LMS van (NGS kit 18); many of these vans were reinforced in this way in BR days. Next is an SR even-planked van, with some of the planking repaired with uneven planks. Finally an SR van has been converted to a banana van by removing the end vents and adding extra door furniture.

designs. Sometimes repairs were done in a different material, for example if a door or part of the end were replaced.

Many more variations are possible. Sometimes sides and ends can be swapped between kits. Look through books of wagons and you will see there are many different designs that can be produced from available kits. Often the main change that is needed is to alter the strapping. Cut off unwanted strapping with a scalpel. Make extra strapping from strips of lead foil (from a wine bottle) with bolt heads pressed into it from the back with a pin – this is best done before cutting out the strip.

COACHES AND MULTIPLE UNITS

Coach kits and kits for multiple units are usually etched metal, and often they are not complete kits, but just the sides and perhaps ends. You are expected to source the underframe and roof, and all the detailed fittings.

If there is a similar RTR coach, the side can be replaced by a new side. This is much easier than building a complete coach. A number of people do such sides, often in etched metal. The ones shown were from Masterclass Coaches, but are not currently available as they were a limited run. Note you need sides that are sized to fit the donor coach: it is no use trying to put a 2mm-scale side on an N-gauge coach, for example.

Choose a donor coach that has interior seating, roof ventilators and toilet filler pipes as close as possible to the new coach. Start by cutting away the windows from the donor coach, leaving just a thin strip near the roof, and the sides below the bottom of the windows. Cut off slightly more than the height of the windows to allow space for glazing to protrude above and below.

File off any raised parts remaining on the sides, such as door handles – an emery board is good for this. Check that no parts of the original side are

Unless a similar RTR coach is available, you have to build the whole coach. These LMS-designed, BR-built, TPO coaches with offset gangways are from Ultima Models (Etched Pixels) components. They have space for a pick-up net, but were never fitted with them, as picking up mail in motion declined after World War II.

Top is the donor coach, a Farish Stanier brake. The existing window surrounds have been cut away, as the new windows are in slightly different positions. However, the brake end windows are identical, so I left these, enabling me to reuse the original glazing. Below are the replacement sides, with cream paint applied.

visible when the new side is placed over it. Clean the etched side by rubbing with a Garryflex abrasive block (grey or brown grit size) to get rid of any tarnish or protective coating.

Add detail such as vents by soldering on etched components. Handles and handrails could be added at this point, soldering from the back. I prefer to glue them on after mounting the sides on the coach, as this makes it easier to add lining decals, and leaves the handles metal coloured, which is usually what you want.

You are now ready to paint the side, as described in a later chapter, and add decals. You might wish to paint the inside the correct colour for the interior, though it is not likely to be noticeable when assembled.

Curve the side to the correct shape to fit the donor coach. Place it on cork or a hard carpet, and roll a metal rod over the back of the side.

You may need to alter the ventilators on the roof, by removing some and adding new ones, and the toilet filler pipes may need changing. Some etches include jigs for drilling the holes for the ventilators.

Glue the glazing on to the back of the side. Check that the side fits in place, with the glazing inside the cut-out part of the side. Glue on the new side using an impact adhesive such as UHU. Make sure it sticks firmly both top and bottom.

LOCOMOTIVES

Unless you are prepared to scratch-build a chassis, you are limited to bodies that will fit an existing chassis. A number of old white-metal kits will fit on Farish chassis – or more accurately, on Farish chassis from twenty or more years ago. There may be a more recent chassis that can be used instead and will have better detail. The quality of the kits is variable: some are excellent sharp castings, but others need a lot of work.

The completed coach. By reusing the glazing at the brake end I retained the bars on the windows. The interior was from the original coach, cut a little to make it fit the window spacing of the new coach.

An LMS unrebuilt Patriot built from a BH Enterprises white-metal kit, on a Peco Jubilee loco chassis. The Fowler tender is another BHE kit, fitted on a Union Mills tender drive.

On the top right is an Asto-Cad 3D-printed model of an unrebuilt Patriot from Shapeways. It is designed to fit the Farish Royal Scot chassis seen below. The tender is a problem as the Stanier tender on the Scot is not correct, but the Scot's tender drive is too big for a Fowler tender. One option is a BHE Fowler tender kit and Union Mills tender drive, as shown on the top left. The other option is to scratch-build one of the larger Fowler tenders used with a few Patriots.

There are 3D-printed bodies that fit RTR chassis: these will be designed to fit a modern chassis.

DETAILING STOCK

N-gauge models used to be basic and lacking in detail; however, that is no longer the case. Most current models only need weathering, and people, loads, and items such as destination boards adding. However, sometimes the only model available is an old one, and it needs detailing to bring it closer to the standard of newer models.

OLD STEAM LOCO MODELS (AND UNION MILLS)

Thirty years ago all models had die-cast metal bodies with handrails that were moulded as part of the body, and only basic details. Wheels were solid. Many have been replaced by newer, better models, but for some the only model is an old one. While it is not usually possible to replace wheels with see-through spokes, most other details can be improved so older models can sit alongside a modern model.

Lamp irons can be made from staples – they are the correct profile and very strong. Drill 0.5mm

This Farish model of an ex-LMS 4F is one of the best recent models. It has many improvements over the previous model from twenty years earlier: wheels that are not only see-through but have very fine spokes, separately applied handrails, and a detailed buffer beam – and not only is there light showing under the boiler, there is also a representation of the inside cylinders and valve gear. The lettering and lining are better, and the writing, only a fraction of a millimetre high, is still readable with a strong magnifying glass.

UNION MILLS

Union Mills is a small company that still produces 'old-style' models of locos with less detailed bodies in cast metal. They do have tremendous haulage: I have seen them pull 150 wagons! Union Mills has produced about twenty-five different locos over the years, all tender locos with no outside valve gear. Most are types that are not otherwise available, so you may want to get them and improve the detail. They only sell direct, and have no web site though they advertise regularly in the *N Gauge Journal*. Their address is Unit 5, Union Mills Trading Estate, Isle of Man, IM4 4AB, telephone 01624 852896.

Union Mills 700 class, in its original condition on the left, except that I have removed the number. On the right, after I have made various improvements:

- A spray of dark grey to reduce the stark black
- Buffer beam repainted a less bright red, and buffer heads painted
- Coupling rod filed thinner to be to scale
- Wheels and coupling rod blackened, and axle end painted black
- Lamp irons added from a piece of a staple
- Vacuum pipe added, a spare from a plastic wagon kit
- Headcode disc added
- Thick wire to tender replaced with shorter, thinner wire so it is no longer visible
- Handrail at rear of cab added
- Valves on top of dome reduced in height
- Fall plate added between cab and tender
- Cab windows glazed

There is plenty of scope for improvements: I could have done more.

The tender needs detailing as well. On this Dean Goods tender I have added brake standards, two handrails, water-tank vents, correctly shaped buffers and a vacuum pipe. All the parts were bought from N Brass.

holes in the buffer beam, centre, and over both buffers. With a pair of fine-nosed pliers, push a short length of staple into the buffer beam. If the hole size is correct no glue should be needed. Similarly attach one at the top of the firebox, this time from a length with a 90-degree bend in it. Southern locos need two more, one each side of the firebox.

If the handrail is moulded rather than separate, it can be cut off and replaced. However, this does mean a complete repaint of the model. A later chapter describes how to add handrails.

Fitting a DCC Chip to Union Mills Locos

Union Mills locos all use a can motor mounted in the tender, so it is easy to intercept the wiring. The motors are very efficient and take little power, so a small DCC chip is fine.

The loco boilers are solid metal, so the chip can't go there. The tender has a lot of metal to give it weight. There isn't space for a socket, but there is room for a small wired-in decoder. The motor is mounted a little off-centre, which means there is a gap down the left into which a chip can be fitted.

For this Union Mills Dean Goods I used the CT DCX76z decoder: it is only 1.7mm thick, and is soldered in directly to avoid the need for a socket. The suppression capacitor and resistor in series with the motor were removed. The chip is stuck to the motor with double-sided tape. This was the first DCC conversion I ever did, and once I had worked out which wire went where, it only took me twenty minutes.

COAL IN TENDERS

Even the best modelled coal on commercial locos doesn't look quite right. Fortunately it is extremely easy to improve it: spread thinned PVA glue over the modelled coal and sprinkle it with finely crushed real coal. There is often a little loose coal behind the coal space, where the water-filler cap is.

Nearly all RTR locos have the tender modelled full of coal. Sometimes this is because the motor and decoder fill the space below. However, if there is space below you can model it only half full of coal (the front will be lower than the back).

PEOPLE

Steam locos with an open cab show off a driver and fireman well. A driver can be put in the cab of a diesel or electric, and a guard leaning on the veranda of a brake van (usually facing forwards – one of his duties was to check the train for loads shifting or signs of a hot axlebox).

Farish makes good ready-painted figures, and Modelu sells exceptionally detailed unpainted figures.

Coaches should have passengers, though they are quite difficult to see, and only those next to the window will be noticed. The figures can be very

The moulded coal load has been cut out, a plasticard floor added, sloped black plasticard glued in at the rear for the back of the coal space, and crushed real coal placed on top, held in place by PVA glue.

Union Mills Dean Goods with driver and fireman added. Details in the cab interior have been painted, the printed number plate has been replaced by an etched metal plate, and brake standards have been added to the tender.

Passengers standing in the corridor of coach show up well. There are several seated passengers, but they cannot be seen as they are too far from the window.

basic. The seated passengers will probably have to be cut off at the waist to get the height correct.

TIE BARS

BR in the 1950s added vacuum brakes to many unfitted wagons. Because the force of the vacuum brakes was greater than hand brakes, they could push the wheels apart, bending the solebars. To counteract this, a strip of metal, a tie bar, was added between the bottoms of the axleboxes. If you have a kit-built wagon on a Peco 10ft chassis it will not have the tie bar, but it is easy to add. Cut off the small raised ridge on the very bottom of the axleboxes with a scalpel. Cut a strip of 0.5mm (0.020in) square plastic the length of the distance between the outsides of the axleboxes (about 24mm), and glue it on the bottom of the axleboxes where the ridge has been cut off. Paint it black.

HEAD- AND TAIL LIGHTS

All trains have to have tail lamps, and before 1976, headcodes. Early headcodes were shown by lamps or discs. In 1960 four-character headcodes were introduced, though steam locos and earlier diesels continued to show the lamp codes. Some trains had to have side lamps on the rear vehicle, for example all unfitted goods trains and earlier passenger trains.

The headcode depends on the region and era you are modelling. It is a complex subject. In the 1950s codes for different train classes were standard. However, the Southern used route-indicating codes instead, as did many local trains in the London area, and the S&D had its own codes. Head lamps on BR(M) were normally painted black, not white, and a few red lamps from the 1930s were still in use on BR(W). If you want more detail, I have written a booklet *Train Lamps and Headcodes* published by the 2mm Scale Association.

Modelu produces very good-looking lamps of various types – they are the best I've seen.

A simple block of plastic cut off 1mm (0.040in) square strip with a dot of red or silver paint looks fine from any distance, and is a lot better than having no lamps.

Southern companies, and occasionally others, used discs instead of lamps during the day. These can be punched out of thin plasticard. Use the 2.5mm setting on a leather punch (available on the internet for a few pounds).

It is possible to add working lamps using 0603 warm white LEDs, which are about the same size as a lamp.

As well as headcodes, expresses on the GWR and LMS often displayed reporting numbers, mainly at weekends and holidays. They were used from the mid-1930s until the end of steam on BR. Sankey Scenics produce printed numbers that can be used for these.

BR(S) used circular section tie bars rather than rectangular ones. They can be modelled using 0.4mm-diameter brass rod, rather than plastic strip. Cut the correct length of rod and squeeze the ends flat in a vice or with pliers. Glue on as for the plastic strip, and paint black.

The brake van has been fitted with a red tail-lamp LED and two warm white LEDs on the sides, painted black in the middle so light is only visible front and back. The rear side has been painted with vermilion oil paint, which is translucent and turns the white into red. Power is picked up from the track.

GANGWAY SHIELDS

On passenger services a cover called a gangway shield was often put over the corridor connectors at the front and back of the train. It was primarily to keep wind and dirt out of the coaches. They were rarely used on parcels trains, and dropped out of use in the early 1970s with the Mk2 coaches. Some RTR coaches, for example the Farish Mk1 coaches, come with shields in the accessory pack. There will be plenty left over for other coaches.

SOUTHERN COACH SET NUMBERS

The Southern Railway and later BR(S) organized most of its coaches into fixed sets of two to twelve coaches, then made up trains by combining sets. The set was identified by a large white number on each end. The Southern Email Group (semgonline. com) has a list of set numbers and the coaches in them at different times. As sets of three or more coaches had a brake compartment at each end, trains often had more brake compartments than other lines. For example, a twelve-coach commuter train made up of three four-coach sets would have six brake compartments. Some Eastern commuter stock was in similar sets.

CHALK MARKS AND POSTERS

Abbreviations for the destination, or dates, or numbers were often chalked on the sides of vans and other wagons. As they only got washed off in time by rain, some vans might have as many as a

Southern Region coach with a set number added. The tail lamp is a length of plastic strip with a red dot.

Left: A van with 'Derby' added with a chalk pencil. Right: A banana van (2mm SA etched kit) with Fyffes poster; an image of the logo is printed on an inkjet.

Vans with posters from Sankley Scenics. They have two different packs. The posters often stayed in place for a long time and became faded, dirty and torn. Tears and other damage can be simulated by attacking the edge with a fibreglass brush, as has been done to the one on the right.

dozen different markings visible. They were hand written, and can be reproduced using a white pencil sharpened to a fine point.

Vans often had posters pasted on the side saying what they contained. Banana vans usually had them for Fyffes or Geest. Other vans that were reserved for a particular traffic had them as well – animal foods and cement were two common products advertised on posters. Another common label was a smaller one saying 'Parcels Mails', and the remains of torn-off labels were common as well. If you have a colour photo, use a package such as Photoshop to

extract it, then size it correctly, and print it on thin paper. Give the sheet a coat of matt spray varnish before use to prevent the colours running, then cut it out and stick it on the side of the van.

WAGON LOADS

Traffic such as coal or ore was usually in one direction, so trains should be loaded one way and empty the other. For a circular layout this happens automatically; it is more work with an end-to-end one. Much the best way to represent coal is to use real

Coal load in a 16-ton mineral wagon.

coal, crushed into small fragments. Put a small lump in a bag, hit it with a hammer, and sieve it, preferably into different sizes. Coal for a power station was usually small pieces, domestic coal medium, and loco coal large.

Use a rectangle of thin black instrument foam as the base of the load, with coal dust scattered on top. Any foam that shows through will look like coal. Put it on top of card or plasticard, with a block of plastic in the middle to raise it to the correct height. By only having the block in the centre you can press

down on one end of the load so the other pops up to remove it. It also saves weight. The top of the coal was usually higher in the centre and often had several peaks resulting from the loading. The number of peaks varied, but all the wagons in a rake would have the same number, having been loaded by the same plant.

A wagon for general goods traffic would rarely travel empty, because when it reached its destination there was usually another load waiting to be sent. Wagons could be quite lightly loaded – it was often preferable to put a load in a wagon on its own so the wagon could be dropped off, rather than mix it with goods for other stations.

Loads could be secured by sheets, chains or ropes. These hardly changed from the early days until the 1980s, when plastic straps largely replaced ropes and chains.

Chains were used to secure heavy loads on flat, bolster and well wagons. When not loaded the chains would often be left on the floor of the wagon.

The photos show a number of materials that can be used to represent rope and chain. They can be attached to suitable points on the wagon with a dab of superglue.

Even the finest chain available looks a little coarse, and it can be difficult to get it to look as if it

Load of planks (wood strip) secured with cotton 'rope'. Wagons loaded like this had the part of the load that was sticking up positioned to the rear, in case the train stopped suddenly.

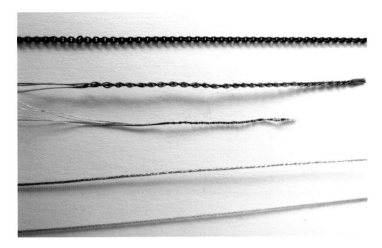

From the top:
- Forty links per inch chain (N Brass)
- Homemade 'chain' made from four strands of 0.2mm tinned copper wire braided together then blackened
- Similar, using 0.1mm copper wire
- Braided stainless steel (0.28mm) from Eileen's Emporium looks like steel rope
- Cotton thread can represent rope.

Four strands of 0.2mm tinned copper wire held in a vice and bent out in four directions prior to braiding together. Take the left and right wires and swap them over, pulling gently upwards and outwards. Then do the same with the top and bottom wires. Repeat until the chain is long enough. The best-looking chain is produced if you always swap one pair of wires so they pass in a clockwise direction, and the other pair so they pass in an anticlockwise direction.

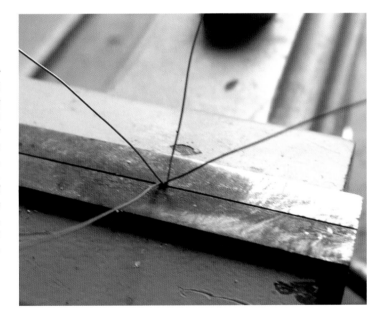

LMS twin bolster wagon (Chivers kit) with a load of H-beam steel (Plastruct H channel painted with Humbrol Metalcote polished steel), secured by chains made out of four-wire braid. The guard needed to keep a close eye on a load like this, as it might shift during the journey, so such wagons would usually be marshalled near the guard's van.

KSA/KTA bogie timber wagons, converted from Roco Cargowagons. The load of timber is secured with blue and orange 'plastic' straps represented by thread. Built by Matthew Knight.

LMS Trestrol wagon (NGS kit) with a sheet-steel load (nickel-silver sheet weathered with rust colours) and secured with forty links/inch chain. Attach one end with superglue, stretch it into position, cut off any excess, then secure the other end. Most machinery wagons had a row of rings along the side, or set into the deck for attaching chains or ropes.

is stretched tight. I prefer to make my own 'chain' by forming a braid out of four strands of thin copper wire – 0.2mm wire from standard connecting wire is ideal, as shown. Colour it black with chemical blackening.

Loads such as crates or barrels can be bought, or you can make your own. Avoid very heavy loads, though, such as a white-metal vehicle. Apart from reducing the number of wagons your loco can pull, very heavy wagons are more likely to uncouple, and can pull lighter wagons off the track on curves. The ideal is for all the wagons to weigh about the same, slightly more for the long-wheelbase ones. If a wagon is very light you may want to add a little more

weight – strips of thin lead sheet stuck underneath with impact adhesive is my preference. For vans, glue a weight inside.

CONTAINERS

Containers are probably under-represented on many layouts. Ventilated and insulated containers largely replaced meat and insulated vans in the late 1950s and 1960s.

Modern containers are fixed to the wagons by special locks at the corners, but older containers were secured by a short chain that included a turn-buckle to tighten it, stored in the pockets on the sides of Conflats when not in use.

A 3-D printed model of a BM (fresh meat) container from Osborn's Models, painted and decals added. Part of an unpainted one appears on the left.

N Brass sells an etch of container chains, enough for four containers. The container chains are the ones with a turnbuckle in the middle and a hook at the end. I blacken them chemically while they are still on the fret. The thin tab on one end can be removed or bent over and inserted into a hole drilled in the wagon.

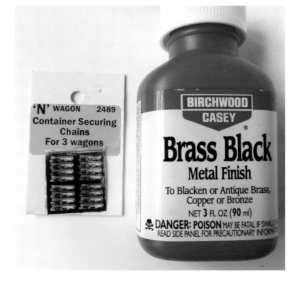

A and BD-type containers (NGS kit) on Peco Conflats, secured by N Brass etched chains. There were rings on each corner of the container, and twelve on each side of a Conflat A, to which chains could be attached. With a single small container the chains would be angled outwards; with a large container, or two small ones, they would angle inwards.

SHEETS (TARPAULINS)

Sheets – the railway term for tarpaulins – were often used over loads in open wagons; perhaps half the loaded wagons would have a sheet. Sheets had three benefits: they kept rain off the load, they prevented a light load such as hay from blowing away, and they reduced theft by hiding the contents and making them more difficult to remove. They hide the load on the model, which makes life easier for the modeller!

Sheets only lasted a few years, so a grouping company sheet would not be seen in the 1950s or later. From World War I onwards sheets were 'common user' – that is, shared between companies. So, for example, a GWR wagon would be as likely to have an LMS sheet on it as a GWR one. Sheets could even form a load in themselves, as 'sheet wagons' visited stations regularly to pick up sheets needing repair and to drop off new ones.

They can be modelled using tissue or cigarette paper. Start by putting a dummy load in the vehicle – a bit of polystyrene foam will do – and cover the wagon in clingfilm. Put the paper over the wagon and hold it in place with a rubber band, low down the side. Adjust it so it looks good. It is best to crumple up the paper first so it looks suitably creased. Spray with diluted wood glue, and adjust the paper if necessary, as it may change shape. When dry, paint it with very dark grey paint. Remove it from the wagon and remove the clingfilm, then cut it off above where the rubber band was. Lettering should be added: a fine-tip white paint pen is good for this.

The lettering is difficult to get looking good, so I prefer to use ready-printed tarpaulins from Smiths, now produced by Scale Link Fretcetera.

The sheet was secured by ropes through eyelets in the edge, usually one at each corner and one in the centre of each side. GWR and SR wagons had cleats on the sides and ends to fix the ropes to, otherwise ropes were secured to anything

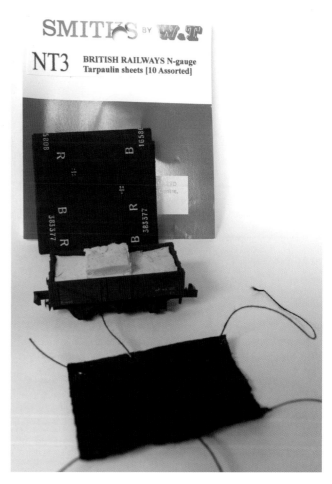

Smith's tarpaulin, printed on thick black paper. I find it too thick, so starting from a corner I peel off the back half of the paper. As when using cigarette paper, crumple it well.

convenient: round the buffer shanks; round door bumpers; through the loops provided at the left end of the solebar for attaching ropes when towing by horse or tractor – but never round brake gear or the coupling hook. Attach lengths of cotton with superglue. Most ropes were tarred, so use black or dark grey. Longer wagons sometimes used two sheets, and a van with a leaky roof might have a tarpaulin over it.

It is possible to buy model loads with tarpaulins over them, but they only look right on flat wagons, because on open wagons the tarpaulin went over the wagon sides, not just the load.

Sheet glued to a wagon, and ropes attached to the buffer shanks.

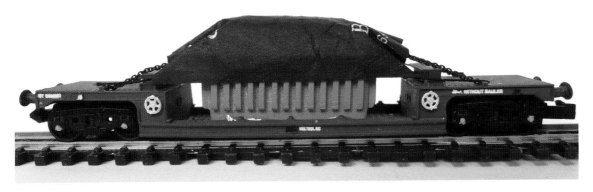

Sheets were used on other wagons as well. This is a Weltrol MC (NGS kit) with a transformer load (Fleetline), held down by chains with a sheet over it.

COUPLINGS

The traditional couplings in British N gauge are Rapido couplings. Just about everything has them as an option. However, they are bulky and obtrusive, and do not look like any prototype coupling. They couple up easily, but are more liable to uncouple than some other types, particularly on slightly uneven track or if not perfectly level in the pocket.

Recent RTR stock has NEM coupling pockets, which allow you to change couplings. The Rapido coupling can be swapped for a buckeye coupling, which is less obtrusive, represents a type of coupling used on many coaches and some goods vehicles, and in my experience is less liable to uncouple. Another advantage of a pocket is that it lets you choose shorter couplings so the gap between vehicles can be reduced. In conjunction with modern close-coupling mechanisms, corridor connections can be made to almost touch. However, note that if vehicles are coupled very closely they might not auto-couple when pushed together. One coupling needs to be lifted over the other to couple, something I find acceptable for stock in fixed rakes.

Both Rapido and Buckeye NEM couplings are available in three lengths, usually termed short, medium and long. Long are the standard ones. This enables you to select ones that give close coupling while still allowing the tightest curves to be traversed. If different lengths are mixed in a rake you must ensure the stock is always put on the same way round and in the same order.

NEM coupling pockets are available separately, so the Rapido socket can be cut off and an NEM one glued on instead.

The couplings can droop or point upwards, which is accentuated by longer couplings, and makes accidental uncoupling more likely. It is sometimes due to moulding flash on the pocket, which can be cured by cleaning it off.

There are tiny differences in coupling pockets and the ends of the coupling between manufacturers, enough that sometimes a coupling from a different manufacturer is not as firmly held as it should be. If near the front of a heavy train the coupling can come out of its socket when running. Try different couplings until you find one that fits tightly.

Couplings that give close coupling on straights can be too close on curves: the buffers press together and cause a wheel or bogie to come off the track. So, after changing couplings, try out the train round the tightest curves and over any reverse curves (a curve in one direction immediately followed by one the other way, such as a crossover). If a mix of coupling lengths is used in a rake, then the stock may only work in one particular order and with everything a particular way round, so mark the stock underneath to show the order it is to go on the track, and the orientation. I usually use the same length couplings at both ends of every coach, but sometimes different lengths for different coaches, so provided the coaches are always in the same order, it doesn't matter which way round they are.

DAPOL EASI SHUNT COUPLINGS

A simple option for automating uncoupling is to use Dapol Easi Shunt couplings: these are a variant of the long established Microtrains couplings. They fit in NEM pockets and can work very well. You can couple up to a long train by reversing gently, but to couple up to one or two wagons you may have to run into them with a little speed.

As well as automatic uncoupling, they have a 'delayed uncoupling' feature. This allows you to uncouple over the magnet, then push the wagons any distance without them recoupling, so you can then move forwards, leaving the uncoupled wagons. The couplings have to move well over to the side for this, however they sometimes fail to move far enough, and they can recouple when pushed over points or round a curve. It is more reliable to have an uncoupling magnet everywhere you want to uncouple.

Easi Shunt couplings. These are short shanks; medium and long shanks are also available. The jaw of the buckeye is hinged, held closed by the small silver spring. The magnetic arm below the jaw pulls it open when it is attracted sideways by a magnet. Below are two wagons coupled up.

Easi Shunt couplings in the 'delayed uncoupling' position, with the claws outside the arm of the coupling opposite. Most NEM pockets allow the coupling to move sideways. If the pocket is rigid or stiff the coupling may not be able to move far enough to get into this position. It will still uncouple, but will recouple immediately it is pushed past the magnet.

The magnet that Dapol offers for uncoupling is large and difficult to disguise, as it needs to be more or less level with the top of the sleepers. Kato couplings are similar, and their uncoupling track works with Dapol couplings, though delayed uncoupling might not work.

An alternative is to use a number of rare earth magnets, either between sleepers, or if they are strong enough, below the sleepers. The magnetic poles must be roughly along each rail, with opposite poles under the two rails. If the edge of the magnet is not close enough to the rail, delayed uncoupling will not work, and ordinary uncoupling may be less reliable. If the magnets are too weak some couplings won't work. If they are too strong, wagons may uncouple when running forwards over the magnets, particularly those near the end of the train.

The tiny springs can pop out if you push in the couplings by the jaw. It is better to grip the shaft with tweezers, or push with a cocktail stick against the inside surface of the buckeye. Dapol provides spare springs with the packs of couplings. A very small drop of glue on the outer end of the spring will help keep it in place. (The same trick works with the type of Rapido coupling that uses a small spring.)

Easi Shunt couplings work well for uncoupling a loco or a few carriages or vans from a train. I would not use them for complex shunting in a goods yard, when one or two wagons often need to be detached.

DG AND BB COUPLINGS

For shunting individual wagons DG couplings work better. They couple easily – you can couple to a single wagon without moving it, and couple on curves. To uncouple you reverse a train over an electromagnet, which is energized as the coupling you want to uncouple passes over. You can push the wagons as far as you want before going forwards and leaving them. This works very reliably, so you only need a single electromagnet to shunt a whole fan of sidings.

The downside is they come as a kit and need to be built, and you need to modify the wagon to fit them. You will probably find the first few tricky to make, but once you have had some practice you can make twenty or so in a session. The kits suggest soldering the iron wire to the end of the loop, but it is easier to make the whole loop from magnetic wire. BB couplings are a compatible alternative with a blackened metal etch. You may find them easier to make. There are a number of videos on the web showing how to build them.

Each coupling has a loop and a hook. When couplings are pushed together the loop lifts over the top of the opposite hook, then drops down on to it. The final part is the latch, a small flap of metal that prevents the loop from recoupling once it is uncoupled. For the most reliable operation, only have a loop on one end of each wagon, otherwise the loops can clash with each other when trying to couple. This means your wagons always need to be the same way round. This is no problem for most layouts, where trains are never turned through 180 degrees, but can be a problem if you use a cassette fiddle yard or have a reversing loop. I usually use a BB coupling for the end with a loop, and a DG for the end with a latch.

Make yourself a height gauge, a block of plasticard 4.5mm high. This goes across the rails to ensure the height is correct. The bottom of the front of the coupling should just touch the block. To test, select a wagon you know works well, couple it to the new

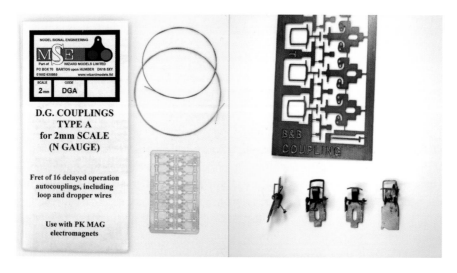

DG and BB coupling kits. Bottom right are assembled couplings, from left to right two views of a BB with loop, a BB with latch but no loop, and a DG with loop.

wagon, and push it by hand over a magnet a number of times to check that it couples and uncouples correctly, and that after uncoupling it can be pushed. A common problem is that the latch stays up so the loop recouples. The latch may need bending slightly to get it to work.

Coupled wagons can be pulled over a magnet without uncoupling provided there is some tension in the couplings; in practice this means that a single four-wheel wagon at the end of a train might uncou-

ple, but two or a bogie vehicle are unlikely to. So if you only want to uncouple at one or two points in the train, for example to uncouple a loco, you can use a permanent magnet rather than an electromagnet. A 3mm-diameter super magnet placed between the sleepers works well and is almost invisible when painted.

As with Easi Shunt couplings, any wagons that always remain coupled can have conventional couplings between them.

Two wagons ready to couple. They are on my 'DG test track', which is a length of straight-set track with a 3mm magnet stuck between the sleepers in the middle.

Coupled up. The loop has gone under the latch and dropped down on to the hook.

Uncoupling. As the wagons are pushed over a magnet it pulls the loop up so it rises above the latch, which lifts to let it pass, then drops down on top of the hook.

Pushed further. The loop drops down, but now rests on top of the latch, so it can't couple to the hook. The wagons can be pushed as far as you want, then when you go forwards they will be left behind.

Provided the couplings are protected from getting bent out of position during transport, I have found DG couplings operate very reliably.

Other designs of automated couplers may be seen, but Easi Shunt and DGs are the most common.

HOOK-AND-EYE COUPLINGS

The Farish 16T mineral wagons pictured are excellent models, accurate and well detailed, but they are let down by the enormous coupling, the pocket that holds it, and too large a gap between the buffers.

As mineral wagons usually run in fixed rakes and do not need to be coupled and uncoupled while operating, a much smaller non-automatic coupling can be substituted.

A hook-and-eye coupling is cheap, and easy to make and fit. All that is needed is brass wire of about 0.45mm diameter, sold by Eileen's and others.

The existing coupling has to be removed. I remove the pocket as well, but you can leave it. On recent Farish wagons the pocket can be unclipped: remove the wheels, undo the two screws holding body and chassis

A pair of Farish mineral wagons with the original Rapido couplings.

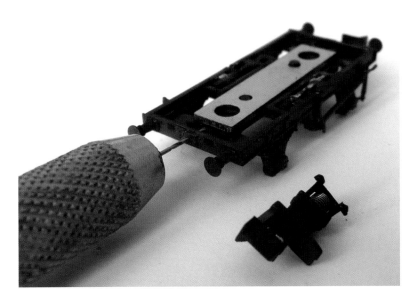

Drill a 0.5mm hole through the centre of where the hook would be; if there is a representation of the hook, as on this wagon, cut it off first, flush with the buffer beam. Make a dent with a sharp point where you want the hole, to guide the drill. The coupling pocket has been unclipped and detached.

To form the 'eye' part of the coupling, bend a loop in the end of the wire using round-nosed pliers. Bend the remaining wire so it goes straight back, then cut it off leaving about 10mm of straight wire.

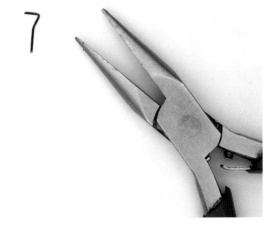

Make the hook part of the coupling by bending 3mm at the end of the wire to just over 90 degrees, and then another slight bend about 4mm further down so the wire is at right angles to the end, as shown. Once you have done a few, this is easy to do by eye.

together, then unclip the coupling pocket by pushing the clips down and towards the centre. On other types of wagon you have to cut off the pocket to remove it.

When on track, the eye should be well below the top of the hook and have at least 1mm of hook below it; if not, bend the hook or eye. I've been using this type of coupling for several years now without any problems, though they do take slightly longer to put on the track.

DUMMY COUPLINGS

If you don't need a coupling on the front of a loco or the rear of a brake van, a dummy three-link or screw coupling as appropriate will look better.

Push the new couplings into the holes in the wagon, and secure with superglue or epoxy. The 'eye' should be positioned so the centre of the hole is in line with the buffer heads. The hook should be slightly in front of the buffer heads: a Peco ballast weight across the buffers makes a good spacer.

Reassemble the wagon: the improvement in appearance is dramatic. When reassembling, the end door and stripe on these wagons was always on the left when looking at the side with the brake blocks.

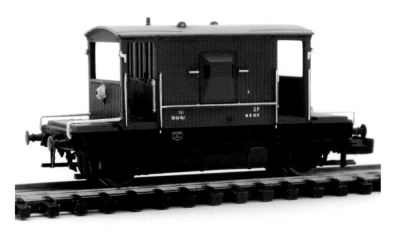

Coupling pocket removed from the brake van, and dummy three-link coupling from a Scale Link fret fitted. The tail lamp is a 0603 red LED, with pick-ups on the wheels for power.

CHAPTER NINE

ROADS AND VEHICLES

ROADS

Most modellers put far less effort into roads than railway track, but there is just as much to model.

Most main roads are quite smooth. I use a matt grey paint on top of card, or thin ply, or 1mm Foamex. If a strip of card is put under the centre so it is higher than the edges, the road can be given an appropriate camber. Tarmac roads are not black, in fact unless wet they are a medium to light grey.

For a rough unmade road, or a track or goods yard, use a base of plaster, modelling clay or grout; this allows you to model anything from a slightly undulating surface to deep ruts and potholes. Paint over it with the approximate colour, and while it is still wet, sprinkle on fine material to give it more surface texture. This can be talcum powder, fine sand (Chinchilla dust), or crushed and sieved ashes. Experiment first on a scrap of ply until you get the effect you want.

Printed roads can be used, for example from Scalescenes, but the joins are hard to disguise, and on most corners you will need to add road markings yourself. Another possibility is very fine wet-and-dry paper, with a wash over to lighten it.

ROAD WIDTH

Many layouts have roads that are too narrow, something that becomes apparent when you put a car down and realize that another car would not be able to pass! Most roads are just about wide enough to have a car parked each side and allow two other cars to pass. The dead-end road outside our house is 25ft (8m) wide with 7ft (2m) pavements each side, so scales to 8cm (a little over 3in).

The station yard on Miller's Dale by Rob Holgate. The base is plaster, painted grey, with sieved ash from a barbecue added. It was weathered with thin washes of slightly different colours, by drybrushing, and with weathering powders. The drystone walls were made from individual flakes of thick paint, glued together, then used as a master for resin casting.

Most roads, particularly in built-up areas, have many patches and repairs. If a cable or pipe has been laid there may be a long, thin strip with occasional wider rectangles. Such repairs can be represented with weathering powders or with paint. Cut out a paper mask to help get the edges straight. Repairs are darker than the main road surface. Round the edge of a patch there is sometimes a thin strip of tar with a few stones that appears much darker. You can model this using a soft pencil, which can be used to add stains and tyre marks as well.

The gutter will often be a darker colour because it has fewer stones, with grates every few yards. Grates look best if inset into the road. Etched metal grates such as those produced by Langley look best. Paint them dark grey and put black paper behind them. Alternatively, draw grates on your computer, print them off and cut them out. Manhole covers can be done in the same way.

A walk looking at similar roads in your area will give you plenty of details to model.

We are used to roads with white lines nearly everywhere, and a great many single and double yellow lines, but these have come in gradually over the years. Roads in the early 1950s would have had very few lines. Aerial photographs show road markings very clearly. There are numerous books and online sites that can provide photographs from the right period and of a similar location.

White lines were used to mark junctions from 1926, and cat's eyes first appeared in 1936, but until the late 1950s most roads didn't have white lines except at junctions. Yellow 'no parking' lines first appeared in 1958, along with parking meters.

I find it easiest to draw lines using a narrow paint pen guided by a ruler, but an alternative is to use laser-cut self-adhesive markings. These include markings such as 'Bus Stop' and 'Slow'.

Road signs were standardized in 1936 as rectangular white signs with a symbol or picture at the top and writing in a box beneath. The posts had black and white stripes and a red triangle on top.

Stoney Lane Depot. The lines on the road are drawn with a paint pen. Note the darker patch of tarmac in the centre of the road. The pavements are card, covered with Scalescenes prints, with plastic strip painted grey for the kerbs.

Various N-gauge vehicles. **Back row, left to right:** *Scania 300-series fire appliance (1988–97) by Jet Flame; Leyland Atlantean bus (1958–72) by Base Toys; and Massey Ferguson 8280 tractor with front-end loader (1999–2003) by Wiking.* **Front row left to right:** *Ford Cortina Mk3 (1970–76) by Oxford Diecast; Toyota Corolla estate (1974–79) by Tomytec; Nissan Fairlady 350Z (2003–2009) by Kawai; Honda Jazz (2001–2008) by Tomytec. Note that some of these, particularly the Japanese ones, were from limited batch runs, and may now be difficult to source or in a different livery.*

Pre-1964 style 'Low Bridge' sign on Wickwar.

In 1964 these were changed to modern signs, in line with continental ones, with no lettering and a cleaner symbol in a red triangle or circle on grey posts. A number of companies sell sheets of signs, or an image may be found on the internet and you can print it off in the correct size.

I make the posts out of strong solid wire, for example 0.6mm or 0.8mm nickel-silver rod. Signs can get knocked: metal posts will bend rather than break, and can be straightened.

VEHICLES

An ever-increasing range of RTR vehicles is available, many highly detailed and extremely well decorated. Manufacturers include Oxford Diecast and Base Toys, who mainly make older vehicles. For more modern vehicles some of the best are Japanese – these are 1:150 scale, rather than 1:148, but this is not significant. Various continental and American suppliers have models but these are 1:160: the difference can be noticeable next to a similar 1:148 model, so be careful where you put them.

The vehicles available cover only a small percentage of designs, and some really common and iconic types are missing. If you want a particular vehicle there may be a kit or a 3D-printed model that you can paint and glaze. However, you are unlikely to save money, as you would with railway wagon kits, and you may have to spend more.

Some older kits have solid windows and are less well detailed than modern models. The windows need painting silver grey, or if the model is metal, my preference is to polish the bare metal, then varnish it. I prefer ones without windows, which have to be glazed.

A model of an express steam loco would not have a gloss finish: it will have a satin finish, because that is what it looks like viewed from a distance. But road vehicles nearly always come with a high gloss finish, and this doesn't look right, particularly next to buildings and rolling stock that are satin or matt.

Give vehicles a coat of satin or matt varnish, and weather them if appropriate. Avoid painting windows, as they will lose their transparency. If the

R Parker does metal car kits mainly from the 1960s/1970s. The three examples shown
are a Ford 7V SWB flat-back (1937–49); a Bedford WLG SWB tipper truck (1931–35);
and a Morris Cowley saloon (1927–30). The detail is good, with open windows that need
glazing. R Parker does not have a web site or email address: you have to find his address
from the internet or an advertisement and write a letter. Gramodels produce a wide
range of military vehicles cast in resin, some of which could be civilian, such as the blue
German Opel Blitz bus (1939–43).

3D printing is ideal for vehicles, and there is an ever-increasing range available. Left
to right: Commer Walk-thru van (1962 to the mid-1970s) by Osborn's Arch Laser; Ford
D800 (1965–1981) by Soehaves Workshop; and finally four by RailNscale: Range Rover
(1970–94), Peugeot 504 estate (1970–74), Ford Escort Mk3 (1980–86) XR3i and BMW
3-series (1975–83).

glazing cannot be removed, either use a brush, or
put small patches of masking tape over the windows
and spray.

When painting kits, as well as giving them a satin
finish, it is best to tone down colours by mixing a
little cream with them. This gives the more muted
colour that is seen when they are viewed from a
distance.

Cocktail sticks are a good way to add details such
as head and tail lamps. As with any painting like this,
check the appearance, and if you are not satisfied, wipe
off the paint with a tissue dampened with thinners.

MOVING VEHICLES

Most layouts have many vehicles, but very few have ones that move. Moving vehicles add another dimension to the layout and always attract attention.

There are at least three systems that people have used to make vehicles move. The simplest is to move a magnet below the road surface so that a magnetized vehicle above follows it. The tractor and trailer on Wenford Bridge shown in Chapter 2 operates in this way. A commercial version is the Magnorail system. One layout that has taken the moving magnet system to another level uses a magnet that can be moved anywhere under a large goods yard, so it can move a tractor to shunt railway wagons. Horses, and later tractors, were often used for shunting in goods yards.

The system most often seen, though still rare, has self-powered vehicles that follow a magnetic wire laid just below the road surface. The Faller system has been available for many years, and more recently, Tomytec produced a similar system. Magnets next to the wire operate magnetic switches in the vehicles to stop and start them, and it is possible to have junctions. You can only have a small number of vehicles moving at once, otherwise the faster ones will run into the slower ones. As each vehicle costs as much as a loco it would be very expensive to model a busy road. However, the Minatur Wonderland HO system in Hamburg has thousands of modified Faller vehicles running under computer control.

The third possibility is a self-powered vehicle with radio-controlled motor and steering. There have been a few layouts with such vehicles in O gauge, but miniature receivers originally developed for model aircraft are now small enough to fit in N-gauge lorries and buses. These vehicles can be steered anywhere on the layout. They can steer in reverse, so they can be driven into loading bays and do three-point turns. The downside is that each vehicle needs its own driver, and total concentration. You have to build the vehicle yourself: complete radio-controlled vehicles are not currently available.

The moving magnet systems are the only ones currently available that can move a very small vehicle such as a car or tractor, though people have scratch-built Faller-style chassis that will fit in a car.

MAGNORAIL MOVING MAGNET SYSTEM

This system consists of a flexible shallow channel that is laid below the road surface in a continuous

A lorry coming out of the Wickwar brewery (Faller) as a coach (Tomytec) passes by.

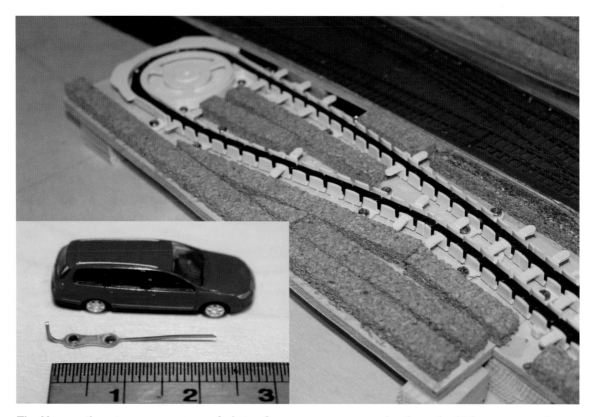

The Magnorail moving magnet system. A chain of magnets moves around a channel, which can go round corners. A thin road surface is put over the top. The motor that powers the chain is at top left. The inset shows a slider with its own magnets. It is dragged along the road surface as the chain moves. The hook fits into any model vehicle with rotating wheels. It is ideal for a busy road with non-stop traffic, as one chain can move many vehicles.

loop. For example, it could go along both sides of a road with a 180-degree bend at each end, off scene. A continuous chain of magnets runs within the channel, powered by a motor. A thin sheet of card covers the channel and magnets, forming the road surface. A magnetic 'slider' is placed on top, which travels round following the magnets underneath. There is a spike sticking up from the slider, on to which a vehicle is placed. Any vehicle with freely rotating wheels will work, and you can have dozens of vehicles running.

FALLER AND TOMYTEC SYSTEMS

In the Faller and Tomytec systems the vehicles are self-powered by a battery and a small motor, and track a buried iron wire. They can be stopped by a magnet to one side of the track, which operates a switch on the vehicle. They travel for a surprisingly long time on one charge, up to two hours.

The Faller and Tomytec systems are not fully compatible, as the Tomytec system uses a more powerful steering magnet and the wire is buried more deeply. It is possible to adjust them so they work together.

THE FALLER CHASSIS

Faller was the first to introduce a road system. The chassis has a motor that drives the rear wheels via a worm gear, with a rechargeable battery to power it. A socket connects to the charger, and a magnetic

Lorry chassis, unmodified except for the replacement cab. A Varta rechargeable battery is on top, the charger socket is at the rear, and the on/off switch at the bottom. The square grey object on the front right of the chassis is a bias magnet to hold the reed switch above it in the 'on' position. A stop magnet under the road cancels out the bias magnet and turns the power off.

reed switch stops the vehicle if over a magnet. The front wheels are on a steering mechanism, guided by an arm with a magnet that sticks out in front, and tracks the hidden wire in the road. There are various vehicles with chassis of different lengths. All are fairly modern continental prototypes, so you will probably want to change the body. In 2020 Faller released a chassis kit with an adjustable wheelbase.

As at an exhibition vehicles are run only part of the time, the battery lasts most of a day. However, it takes about twelve hours to recharge, so at a two-day exhibition you have to recharge it over-night, which is inconvenient if you have several vehicles. You can buy a sophisticated electronic charger from Faller that will recharge in an hour without overcharging, but it costs over £100.

An alternative is to replace the rechargeable battery with a disposable battery, usually an LR44

button cell. They are smaller, so fit more vehicles, provide similar speeds to the rechargeable battery, and last for about half a day at an exhibition. Buy the cheap alkaline batteries: the more expensive and higher capacity silver and zinc/air versions cannot handle the current draw and don't work. You will need to make your own holder for the battery.

THE TOMYTEC CHASSIS

More recently Tomytec produced a similar but slightly different system. The first version used two disposable batteries; I prefer the later version

The Tomytec chassis, with a replacement Faller-style steering arm and lights added on the front. It is recharged via the USB socket on the bottom – twenty minutes' charging is sufficient for two hours' running. The chassis is adjustable between a 29mm and 38mm wheelbase. Version WMB-L01 has 6.2mm wheels, WMB-L02 6.5mm.

Top: *The Tomytec steering arm.* Centre: *A spare Faller steering arm, bent and filed to match the Tomytec arm, with a pin soldered on.* Bottom: *The replacement arm fitted to a Tomytec chassis.*

with a rechargeable battery. The chassis is much more sophisticated than the Faller, with a micro-chip controller that allows it to start gradually and switch between fast and slow. It has front and rear lights, and the brightness of the rear lights increases when stopping. The downside is that it is substantially bigger than the Faller chassis; it will only fit into buses and coaches, and only then if the front axle is set back at least 7mm from the front of the vehicle.

The Tomytec chassis is designed to follow a wire buried slightly deeper than the Faller, and if an unmodified chassis is used on Faller track the steering magnet tends to stick to the wire. Faller sell weaker replacement magnets, but these are for the earlier version of the chassis. On the later version, the steering magnet is cylindrical and a tight fit inside a plastic tube. If pushed up about 1mm, it will work on the Faller track. The exact position is critical – move it too far and it will not follow the wire. I prefer to replace the arm with a Faller-style arm made from a spare Faller arm, or from phosphor-bronze strip and a small magnet.

DESIGNING THE TRACK

The main constraint is the turning circle of the vehicles. The minimum radius for Faller vehicles is about 3in (8cm), though a little more is better, and it helps to ease into it gently with a transition curve. Tomytec will manage a rather tighter curve, down to about 2in (5cm).

Two routes can cross: provided the angle is 45 degrees or more the vehicles will pass over the join. If the angle is less than 45 degrees, leave a gap in both wires for a few millimetres each side. Similarly, it is possible to go across railway track. In both cases, try to provide a few inches of straight track before the crossing so the vehicle is stable.

The depth of the wire is critical. It must not stick up, nor must the top of the wire be below the road surface: if the wire is even 0.5mm below the road surface you may get problems, particularly on curves.

Board joins need particular care. If the join is not level the steering arm may catch. The wires on each side of the join need to line up. The Tomytec chassis is more sensitive to errors than the Faller.

The road surface must be smooth, hence my preference for using thin ply as a base. Any changes in slope should be fairly gentle, though the vehicles will go up steep hills, certainly 1 in 7. The Tomytec is more sensitive to small bumps and bits of grit stuck in the paint than the Faller. Go over the road surface with very fine wet-and-dry paper after the paint has dried.

The wire is laid by cutting a shallow groove in a ply road surface and gluing it in with superglue, then painting over with Faller paint. There is 'Set Track' available in the form of laser-cut ply, but I prefer to be able to lay the road in the exact shape I want: it is a lot cheaper, and easy to retrofit or modify!

I use an Olfa plastic cutter (available from many model shops) to make the groove; however, a specialized electric cutter can be bought from Faller.

The wires need to be at least 20mm apart to allow vehicles to pass each other, and rather more on curves. Try positioning two of your wider and longer vehicles, noting that the rear end tends to be inside the line of the wire when going round a curve. The biggest vehicles we have are based on Oxford Diecast coaches and the Tomytec chassis.

Remember to leave space at the sides for the pavement, particularly on the insides of bends. Allow for a Tomytec chassis, which is wider than the Faller.

The road can be painted with the grey paint that Faller supply – this is quite thick so fills gaps, hiding the wire.

Vehicles sometimes fail to follow the wire, so add a small lip to any baseboard edges they might reach to prevent them dropping on to the floor.

STOP MAGNETS

To stop vehicles I use permanent magnets under the track, moved in and out of position by a servo motor. They need to be lowered by about 15mm, though the amount depends on the magnets used. I used 5mm-diameter, 3mm thick super-magnets.

Because the Faller mechanism was designed for driving on the right, the stop switch is on the right-hand side of the vehicles. If vehicles drive on the left this means the stop magnet is towards the centre of the road, and is likely to stop a vehicle going in the

The mounting of the magnets on the servo can be very simple and crude. The magnet is attached to a bracket on the servo arm, and the servo is screwed to the underside of the ply road.

Stop the bus! I took a second wire from the servo operating the stop magnet at the bus stop to wave the arm of the woman standing there, so she signals for the bus to stop. This was simple to do but attracts plenty of attention at exhibitions. The next job is to make her 'get on the bus' (disappear into a hole while hidden by the stopped bus).

other direction as well. To prevent this happening, have the guide wires at least 4cm (1.5in) apart at stopping places. If you are only using Tomytec, the magnet can be used the opposite way round and on the left of the guide wire.

The stop magnet should be positioned roughly in line with the right-hand side of the vehicle. On curves the position may need adjusting, as the vehicles tend to travel slightly inside the guide wire.

Vehicles differ in sensitivity, so check the stop magnet works with all your vehicles. Tomytec reacts to a magnet further away from the wire than Faller, but will not react to one that is quite close

to the wire. If the magnet is positioned close to the wire you risk affecting the steering arm.

JUNCTIONS

It is possible to have multiple routes, and to select the route to be followed at junctions. At the point where the routes diverge, leave an 8mm gap in the wire; beyond this the wires for the two routes should be 2–3mm apart. Mount a small movable magnet (say, 2mm in diameter and 2mm thick) under the gap, with the pole that attracts the magnet on the steering arm uppermost.

Joining two routes is easy. Have one wire continuous, and take the other to within a few millimetres

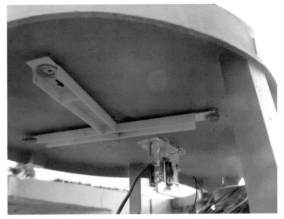

The magnet under the junction. The pencil lines show where the guide wires are. The magnet can move about 2mm, to be in line with one route or the other; a servo or wire in tube can be used to move it. You may need to experiment a little with the exact position and the strength of the magnet to get it to work reliably. Rather than fixing the magnet to the mounting, have a small square of tinplate on the mount and place the magnet on to it. This lets you move the magnet around to find the ideal position, and you can experiment with different sized magnets.

at a shallow angle; when the vehicle comes to the end of its wire it will continue in the same direction, then pick up the other wire.

The 'Taxi Rank'

We wanted to be able to hold at least two vehicles in the off-scene turning loops, and came up with a simple mechanism of magnets on a rotating arm. We used a servo to rotate the arm. The magnets are on steel washers glued to the arm, so we can remove a magnet if we want fewer stop positions.

This worked quite well, and we used it for several years at exhibitions. However, if you sent out two vehicles at once, you had to remember to move one forwards by hand, and operators often forgot. So we built a far more complex automated shuffle, which detects when vehicles are present and moves them forwards if there is space.

All the roadway controls, including junctions and bus stop, are controlled from a tablet that connects

The arm is the width of the loop under the road and pivoted in the centre, with a magnet at each end of the arm just inside the guide wire. A vehicle stops over the first magnet. When the arm is rotated backwards a short distance the vehicle is released and moves on to the next magnet. The arm is returned to its original position and the vehicle follows the magnet forwards. Each time the arm is operated the vehicle advances one magnet position, and when released from the front one it sets off along the road.

via WiFi to a web server running on a Raspberry Pi computer. The operator can stand in front of the layout, and watch each vehicle. It is much easier than fixed controls and lets you talk to the public. All our operators enjoy running the road system at exhibitions. An old router provides the WiFi connection.

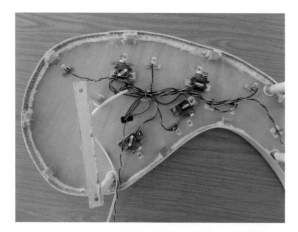

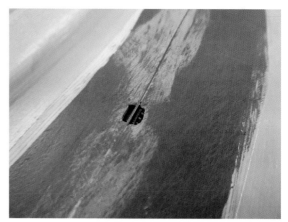

Four Hall-effect detectors, H1–H4, mounted immediately below the guide wire (as shown above) detect the magnet on the steering arm as a vehicle passes. An Arduino computer, in the plastic box on top, takes this information and uses it to drive the four-stop magnet servos (M1–M4) to shuffle vehicles up. An interface between the Arduino and CBUS takes commands from the operator to release vehicles, and passes back information on the position of vehicles to display on the control screen.

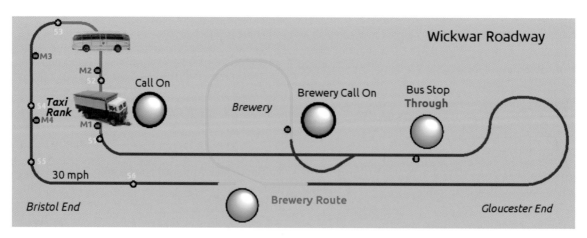

JMRI was used to produce the control screen for the road. It is displayed on the tablet or phone used by the roadway operator. Any device with WiFi and a browser can be used. Images of the parked vehicles are displayed, identified by an RFID detector at the start of the taxi rank.

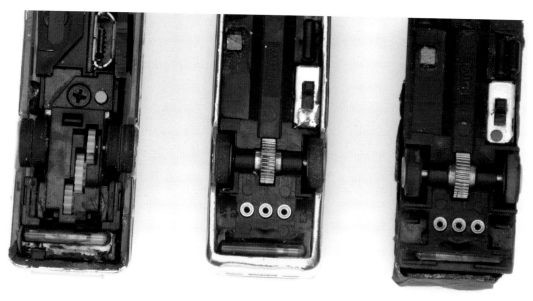

The glass-encapsulated low-frequency RFID transponders are only 12mm long and 2.1mm in diameter. They fit behind the rear bumpers of the vehicles.

TOMYTEC SPEED CONTROL

The Tomytec chassis has two speeds, and switches between them when it goes over a suitable magnet – either opposite polarity to a stop magnet on the right of the wire, or the same polarity as a stop but on the left of the wire. If at a bus stop a magnet is placed a few inches before and after the stop, the bus will slow down as it approaches, and then resume normal speed when it has gone past.

MAINTENANCE

If anything is slightly wrong with the vehicles, particularly the steering, they will fail to track the wire and will veer off into a hedge or one of the buildings by the road. Maintenance is vital.

When you pick up a vehicle it is easy to push a tyre sideways so it is not straight on the wheel, and this will usually prevent it steering properly. The Faller ones are very prone to this, so check them every time you put them on the road. A little glue on the wheel rim can help.

Vehicles will pick up fluff and hair, which gets wrapped round the axles or gear, and it doesn't take very much to stop the wheels turning freely and slow the vehicle down. Run a vacuum cleaner over the road

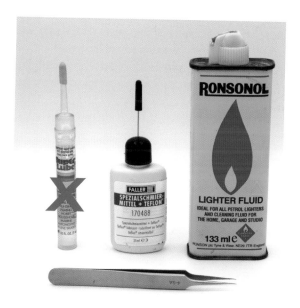

Do not use oil on the vehicles, particularly the steering mechanism: it can go sticky and make the steering stiff; instead use the special Teflon lubricant that Faller sell. If the steering or rear axle has got gummed up, wash it with isopropyl alcohol or lighter fluid, then wobble the steering around, and re-lubricate it. If this doesn't work, take the steering unit off (withdraw the pin at the front on Faller), disassemble and clean thoroughly. As a last resort a replacement steering mechanism can be bought.

The end of the steering arm on Faller vehicles should rest flat on the road. Put it on a plastic box lid and view it with your eye level with the road surface to see how flat it is, bending if necessary. Even more importantly, the arm must be able to move up and down to cope with uneven roads. The screw that holds it on should be quite slack; check the arm has about 1mm of movement up and down, bending it if necessary. The magnet is attached to a bent-over flap at the end of the arm: by raising this flap the effect of the magnet can be reduced if it is sticking to the guide wire.

before each session. After every running session clean hairs off the axle and gears with fine pointed tweezers. If this is difficult, pull the wheel off the axle and clean the axle, then push the wheel back on.

The wheels can become loose on the axles. A dab of superglue inside the wheel may fix it (clean the wheel and axle first to remove any grease or lubricant). If that doesn't work, buy replacement wheels.

TEST TRACK

I recommend building a small test track. A piece of ply about 9 × 18in (22 × 45cm) makes a good base. You can practise laying the wire and road before starting on the layout, and can test slopes and junctions to make sure they work. Afterwards it is useful for testing vehicles and for demonstrating how the system works.

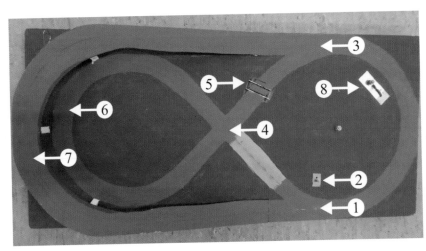

My test track: (1) junction (diverging), with magnet underneath; (2) lever to move magnet; (3) tracks joining; (4) roads crossing; (5) road crossing railway track; (6) a tight 3in (7.5cm) radius curve, and (7) a more generous 4in (10cm) radius on a bridge; (8) stop magnet underneath road, which can be moved backwards by the lever to release a vehicle.

REPLACEMENT BODIES

All the Faller vehicles represent fairly modern German vehicles, and you will probably want to replace the vehicle bodies with something more appropriate. Plastic bodies are best, as a metal body is more difficult to modify, and the extra weight will slow the vehicle down and decrease the running time. It is easiest if the body matches the wheelbase of the chassis you want to use, but it is possible to alter the wheelbase.

We operate four vehicles at a time on the layout, out of ten different vehicles we have available. You need spare vehicles to allow for ones recharging, and there are usually one or two that are 'acting up' and not usable.

When replacing the cab, positioning is critical – it needs to be square on to the front wheels, and just clear of the wheel arch. It may take a couple of attempts to get it right, as the tolerances are very tight. You may have to file a little off the wheel arches: it is essential that the steering can move without the wheels touching the wheel arches. I use gel superglue to give me time to adjust its position.

Base Toys Beaver Flatbed. The replacement cab was fitted as before. The flatbed from the model replaced the rear of the original lorry. It needed a hole cutting where the top of the motor sticks up. Because I wanted most of the flatbed to be visible, I replaced the rechargeable battery with a button cell. A 2mm-diameter super-magnet is embedded in the truck bed with a thin wire soldered underneath to act as one connection to the battery, and to hold it in place. (Cheap LR44 cells are magnetic, though I later found that the top of the Duracell version is not!) The other contact is thin phosphor-bronze wire pressing on the sides of the button cell. A 'crate' made from planked plastic sheeting fits over the battery. The other 'crate' is a lead weight.

Base Toys Albion lorry: a simple conversion of the Faller truck. The original cab was removed and the cab from the Albion glued on. The body of the van, a plastic cover over the battery, was replaced with one that looked like a tarpaulin. I cut a block of foam to the correct size, then covered it with cigarette paper and strands of cotton to represent ropes. Superglue was added to the outside to make it rigid, taking care not to glue it to the foam. A thin layer of epoxy resin on the inside gives further strength.

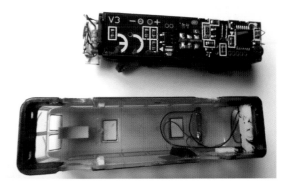

Oxford Diecast Burlington Seagull. The coach has a plastic body (a few early Oxford vehicles have metal bodies). Remove the pillar in the centre of the vehicle. Cut most of it off, then remove the remainder with a burr in a mini-drill. Adjust the chassis length to match the vehicle by loosening the adjusting screw. Then glue suitably sized pieces of plasticard strip to the inside of the vehicle, to make the chassis a push-fit into position, and add spacers above so it is the correct height. The steering magnet needs to be adjusted for the Faller track.

Two coaches on Tomytec chassis with head- and tail-light LEDs added.

The LEDs on the chassis can be connected to the headlight/tail lights by light guides. We did this in one conversion, but they are not very bright. In the vehicle pictured, the two LEDs on the chassis have been replaced by four 0603 LEDs. The two front ones are mounted on the front of the chassis; the two rear ones are in the body, with phosphor-bronze wipers in contact with a strip of PCB glued to the roof for power. The area around the LED is painted black inside to stop light showing through the body. The paint over the lights on the outside was removed by gentle scraping with the tip of a scalpel blade.

RADIO-CONTROLLED VEHICLES

The Faller and Tomytec car systems let you run vehicles along a route and can even manage junctions, but they cannot reverse, and they only run where the guide wire has been laid. A radio-controlled vehicle can go along any road on any layout, and can steer in reverse to get into loading bays. But there is a downside: while you can set a train or a Faller vehicle moving and do something else for a while, driving a radio-controlled vehicle needs total concentration.

SELF-PROPELLED WAGONS

Some goods yards had small wagon turn-tables, over which individual wagons were moved using ropes and capstans. The photo of Queen Street Goods in Chapter 2 has several on the left. A van could be fitted with a receiver, a battery, and a small motor so it could move on its own.

Deltang produces miniature receivers, originally for model aircraft, but they also have versions for controlling vehicles. Micron Radio Control stocks Deltang and other components such as batteries and actuators for the steering. The receiver is 11.8 × 12.9 × 2.2mm. I decided I could fit this and the other components in a Base Toys Albion CX box van, which is quite a small lorry. Batteries come in various sizes, and a 100mAh one just fits in the top of the van body and will run the vehicle for around an hour, recharging in about an hour.

Completed van with radio control; the transmitter is behind.

A Faller chassis can provide steering, motor, gears and wheels (though the example in the photos uses a motor and gearbox from Mikro Antribe). Remove the existing battery, reed switch and associated bias magnet. Add the receiver board and a LiPo battery. Connect the battery via a Picoblade socket for easy removal, as these batteries will need replacing after a few hundred recharges. You may prefer to remove the battery for charging and safe storage – LiPo batteries can catch fire if they develop a fault. There should be a resettable fuse in series with the battery; it is little thicker than a wire. The battery is connected via the switch to the receiver.

The motor needs to be connected to the receiver output. If you connect it directly, it will go from stationary to maximum with only a small movement of the knob, making control difficult. The power needs to be reduced: I found two pairs of back-to-back diodes in series gave the best result, better than adding a resistor.

Finally you need to be able to control the steering. In a larger scale a servo could be used, but even the smallest are too big for N. Fortunately there is a much smaller device called an actuator. It comprises a coil of wire, inside which pivots an arm with a magnet on it. A magnet glued to the side of the coil holds the arm straight. When a current flows through the coil, the arm moves left or right depending on the direction of the current, and the greater the current, the more it moves. As supplied, the actuator is too sensitive and quite weak, so steering is erratic. The strength can be increased, and the sensitivity reduced, by increasing the size of the magnet on the side of the coil. I found that adding a magnet 3mm in diameter and 1mm thick was about right.

The actuator has to be mounted near the front and connected to the steering. It will just fit in the cab of the Albion lorry. I built a front end out of metal to take it and the Faller steering. With a slightly larger vehicle it could have gone on top of a Faller chassis.

The lorry and all the components in it cost just under £100; the transmitter and charger cost just under £70, and could be used with other vehicles or projects.

Chassis with receiver mounted. The battery (top) is connected via a plug for easy replacement. Similarly, the steering actuator is connected by the plug in the centre.

Steering actuator. A brass sleeve fits over the actuator arm, and a wire, soldered into it, connects to the steering via a loop in the end, which goes over a pin in the Faller steering bar.

CHAPTER TEN

PAINTING AND FINISHING

PAINTING

PREPARATION

Painting is easier if the model is in separate parts, with each part painted a different colour: for example the underframe, body and roof of a coach. Build it in sections, and only do the final assembly after painting. I prefer to glue the handles and handrails on to coaches after applying lining decals, so they are not in the way; besides, you often want to leave them unpainted.

Cheap ultrasonic cleaners are sold for cleaning jewellery, and this size is fine for N. They are particularly good for cleaning soldered kits prior to painting, but can be used on plastic kits as well. Beware of using them on models assembled using superglues – they can clean the glue off and leave you with a set of parts.

All traces of flux must be removed from soldered kits before painting, otherwise it will react with the metal over time and cause the paint to bubble and flake. If you have an ultrasonic cleaner, use that; alternatively scrub with an old toothbrush and dilute detergent – Flash is good because it is slightly alkaline, which will help neutralize the acidic flux. Paint will not adhere well to sharp corners, and is more likely to chip off them, so blunt any sharp metal corners with fine wet-and-dry paper before painting.

3D-printed models often need special cleaning – for example, those from Shapeways may have traces of wax. Follow the supplier's instructions.

Resin castings may have release agent on them. Scrubbing with toothbrush and dilute detergent or washing-up liquid will remove them. There may be mould lines on resin castings: remove these with a knife or fine abrasive paper.

Use fine wet-and-dry paper to clean up and polish models. A small square is enough for most jobs, so a full sheet lasts a long time. Use extra fine (800 grit) to super fine (2,000 grit). To get into a tight location, glue some on to a narrow strip of plastic or wood to make a small emery board. For hard materials, or to get the smoothest finish, wet the paper before starting, and wash the paper during sanding to clean off the slurry. For a final polish, toothpaste works well.

All models should be washed to remove grease, as this may stop the paint adhering properly. Isopropyl alcohol (IPA) diluted 10:1 with water is good, and works better than more concentrated IPA. Wash, then wipe dry with a paper towel. Alternatively use a dilute detergent such as Flash, but rinse it off thoroughly.

Use disposable gloves to prevent leaving fingerprints after cleaning and before spraying. Buy powder-free ones, to avoid getting powder on your models. There are tight-fitting ones made from a variety of rubbery materials: nitrile, latex, vinyl. Clear, looser gloves made of a hard plastic and intended for food preparation are a fraction of the price. They are adequate for holding a model while spraying, but not as good for delicate work, when latex gloves are the best.

PRIMING

Priming is applying a thin layer of special paint that adheres well to the model. It often doubles as an undercoat, to provide a uniform colour on which to apply other colours. If you don't need an undercoat, a very thin semi-transparent layer of primer will suffice. The more paint that is added, the more small details get covered up.

For brass and nickel-silver etched kits use an etch primer, which contains acid, to etch into the metal, giving better adhesion. These are sold for car repairs.

For all other materials I use Halfords' spraycans of primer. I use grey for most models, but red oxide

The primers I use most: Halfords' grey or red oxide for plastic or white metal, and etch primer for brass and nickel-silver kits.

if the model is to be maroon or bauxite, and white is also available. If you intend weathering wagons, the grey and red oxide primers on their own are a good approximation to BR grey and bauxite.

Priming often shows up minor defects in the model, such as an uneven joint or a gap. Sand or fill these after priming if necessary. 3D prints can have minor irregularities that the primer highlights, and that need sanding smooth – but beware of damaging fine detail when doing this. Sometimes you will need to prime and sand more than once, in effect using the primer as a thin filler.

PAINTS AND PAINTING TECHNIQUE

Whether painting by brush, spraycan or airbrush, several thin coats are better than one thick coat, even if it takes a little longer. Fine detail will not be covered up as much, and the finish is likely to be smoother. It is better to slightly over-thin the paint than have it too thick.

In general, assuming that you have the equipment and skills, painting with an airbrush will give the best finish. However, good results can be obtained using a brush or spraycans.

Paints come in two main types: enamel paints, which are solvent-based; and acrylic paints, which are water-based. Find a brand and a type of paint you are happy with. Ask others for recommendations – most people have paints they 'get on with'.

Don't worry about getting the exact colour. There is no 'correct' colour, for a whole variety of reasons:

- Paints fade over time.
- Dirt and pollution change their colour.
- Usually an N-gauge model is viewed from a scale 100 yards away, and at this distance colours appear less vivid. If I have the 'correct' colour, I mix some cream with it to dull it down and lighten it. This is sometimes referred to as 'scale colour'.
- Until relatively recently, paints were hand mixed by the railways, so every batch would be slightly different. And colours could vary between different workshops: the Western Region version

HALFORDS' SPRAYCANS

I use these for most of my painting – they are reasonably priced, good quality, and the nozzles do not get clogged up as much as some other spraycans. There is a wide range of colours, but they are named after cars, so you need to know the equivalents. Here are some:

GWR/BR Loco Green	Land Rover Bronze Green or Ford Laurel Green
GWR Coach Cream	Rover Primula Yellow
GWR Freight Grey	Rover Tempest Grey
BR Coach Carmine	Ford Rosso Red
BR Coach Cream	Vauxhall Gazelle Beige
BR Coach Cream – well worn	Peugot Antelope Beige
BR Loco Yellow Warning Panel	Vauxhall Mustard Yellow
BR Diesel Light Green Band	Ford Highland Green
BR Diesel Blue	VW Pargas Blue or Ford Fjord Blue
BR Steam Blue	Peugeot Royal Blue
BR/LMS Red	Rover Damask Red
SR Dark Olive Green	Land Rover Consiton Green
Roof Grey	Halford Plastic Bumper

The finish is gloss, which is an advantage as decals are best put on a gloss surface.

of the crimson in the pre-1956 livery was more orange than on other regions.

- If a model is to run with RTR models in the same livery, you want a close match to them, and not 'accurate' colour.

I have a few common railway colours. If I need something else I mix colours, starting with one that is close, and adding other colours to adjust it. I use the aluminium trays that mince pies come in to mix small quantities of paint. Stir the paint with wooden

Six coaches in BR crimson and cream livery. While there was variation in the colours of the prototype, it was probably not as much as these show. The three on the left are all Farish MK1 coaches from different eras. On the right is a Dapol Gresley, a Dapol Collett and a Farish Hawksworth.

My Badger electric paint stirrer mixes paint quickly. It is gentle enough not to splash, even with small tins, provided you are careful to switch it off before lifting it out of the tin. For cleaning brushes I have a jam jar with about an inch of brush cleaner. The cleaner lasts for years before you need change it, as the paint settles out, on to the bottom. To clean the paint stirrer, put it in the jar and turn it on for a few seconds.

toothpicks or cocktail sticks, then put a few drops of each colour on to the pie tray in separate areas. Mix to the colour needed with a paintbrush. You can buy large boxes of wooden toothpicks that are sold for craft work.

When two colours need to be applied, spray the whole model with one first, then mask over it and spray the second colour. The second colour has to cover up the first, so spray the one that has the greater covering power second. You may want to experiment on a bit of plastic first: yellows and creams are often poor, and some reds are semi-transparent.

Do not use decorator's masking tape as it is likely to take off paint when it is removed. Use specialized tape: I recommend Tamiya masking tape. Allow at least a day for the first coat to dry and harden before applying the masking tape. Press the edge of the tape down firmly. Sometimes paint can bleed under the edge, but you can avoid this by sealing it with a thin coat of clear varnish before spraying the new colour.

Remove the masking tape as soon as you finish spraying. Do not pull it at right angles to the side – instead, pull off one end, then pull parallel to the side with the tape doubled over: this makes it less likely that paint under the tape will lift off. If you don't remove it immediately the paint will have hardened and it is more likely that you will pull bits

The strip in the centre is to remain cream, while the rest is sprayed red. Two strips of Tamiya tape have been applied, one lined up with the top of the cream area and the other with the bottom. The tape must be narrower than the total width to be masked, but wider than half. For very wide areas, use paper to mask the centre.

off. Worse, if any paint has crept under the tape it will be difficult to remove, while if dealt with immediately it can be removed with a clean brush dampened with thinners. Often you will be applying lining decals over the join, which means that small bleeds or irregularities in the line will be covered up.

CHEMICAL BLACKENING

Chemical blackening turns metals black or a very dark brown. It works on most metals, including brass, nickel silver, solder and steel. It doesn't work on stainless steel. It has many advantages over painting: it is easier and faster, it does not obscure fine detail, and the result is hard-wearing. For blackening metal couplings it is essential, as paint will stop them working. There is no risk of messing up paint already applied, and if you do get it on some metal that was intended to be bare, it is easily removed with a fibre brush.

If only a little blackening is applied, you can get a lighter brown, which gives a good rusty/dirty oil effect – for example on coupling rods or part of a crossing V.

It can be a good idea to blacken metal before painting it a dark colour, particularly for protruding parts where the paint is likely to get knocked off, as the black will be much less noticeable than bare metal. It acts as a primer for the metal.

I use Birchwood Casey Super Blue for any metal. Many model shops sell it, and it is widely available on the internet. I have tried other ones, supposedly better for particular metals, but have not had better results.

It is vital the metal is absolutely clean, otherwise it will not blacken properly. First go over it with a fibreglass brush or wirewool and scrub thoroughly, being particularly careful to remove any adhesive or rosin flux. Then clean off any grease by washing with Flash or diluted IPA.

Dip a cotton bud in the blackener to apply it. The metal will gradually darken; add more if needed. It can look dark brown rather than black, but it will get darker when it is fully dry and hard. If a patch remains bright, just clean that area with a fibre brush and repeat. When dark enough, wash off any remaining liquid with water, and dry by dabbing with a paper towel. Do not rub, as the blackening is quite soft at this stage. Wipe it with a cloth or cotton bud moistened with ordinary mineral oil (3-in-1). The oil helps the blackening harden. Leave it for a day before handling. The chemicals are poisonous, so store them securely, and wash your hands after use.

In theory the blackened metal is conductive, so loco wheels can be blackened. However, in practice I find it can make pick-up and running poorer. Conductivity can be improved by polishing the blackened metal with a clean cotton bud after it has hardened. If this doesn't work, remove the blackening from pick-up areas with a fibreglass pen.

DECALS

Nearly all the decals available will be water-slide decals. They are stuck with water-soluble glue to light blue backing paper, which must be soaked in order to release the decals. There is usually a transparent layer – the carrier – over the markings. For example, a loco number will have carrier between the digits to form a single decal. The carrier should not extend much beyond the printing, as it will show up and may prevent you from positioning the decal close to raised detail. Fortunately most sheets only have the carrier where essential. However, if the carrier covers the whole sheet you need to cut out the decal as close as possible to the lettering.

Applying blackening to the brass buffers of a van using a cotton bud.

There are important differences, depending on how they are printed: they may be screen-printed, ALPS/OKI printed, or printed with UV-cured inks.

Screen-printed: Most of the larger companies produce decals in this way. The colours are printed on to a sheet covered in glue, then a transparent layer – the carrier – is printed over the top. Most sheets are printed with only the minimum amount of carrier, but a few have the carrier over the whole sheet. You can tell where the carrier is by looking at the sheet at a shallow angle with light reflecting off it. The carrier will show up, as it reflects the light differently.

ALPS/OKI printed: ALPS-brand computer printers are unusual as they print solid opaque colours, and hence can produce decals. Despite not having been made since 2010 a number of small companies, such as Cambridge Custom Transfers, still use these printers, as they are ideal for small runs. The paper they are printed on has carrier all over on top of a glue layer. The writing is printed on top. The printing on top of the carrier film is quite soft and is easily damaged – for example, pulling a fingernail across can damage lettering. If you buy this type of decal, *immediately* spray the whole sheet with two coats of matt or satin spray varnish before handling it. This will protect it from damage when the decals are applied.

Digitally printed with UV-cured inks: This is a newer technology, used by Railtec and others, and it will probably replace screen printing in time. It uses high-end computer printers. The ink is hardened immediately by UV light and is very tough. A transparent layer is only needed where there are separate letters to be joined together to form one decal: solid colour, such as white letters on a black patch, needs no carrier. They can be treated like the screen-printed ones except that decal softening liquids (*see* below) do not work on them, as there is no conventional carrier film. They differ from screen-printed decals in having a matt finish, rather than a glossy one.

All decals should be applied to a gloss surface, or at worst satin. A matt surface at a microscopic level is rough so it does not reflect light: this roughness means that decals do not stick well. Worse, tiny air bubbles become trapped under the decal and make the 'transparent' parts a silver grey. If necessary paint where the decal is to go with a clear varnish such as Pledge floor polish. Usually two or three coats are needed.

Renumbering. Often you want to change the number or crest on a loco. To remove the existing number, use a scalpel held at right angles to the model, and push it very gently across the number. Do not apply pressure – use a lot of light strokes.

When I have removed almost all the decal I go over it with a wet ink eraser sharpened to a point. The ones in the form of a pencil are easiest to use. Practise first on an old wagon. After applying the new decals you need to apply varnish. Either spray the whole loco, or you can paint varnish that matches the original finish over a smaller area, for example the cab side. If a cabside number ends up looking cleaner that the rest of the loco that is fine, as they were often cleaned with a wipe of an oily rag.

MAKING UP NUMBERS

Sometimes you need a particular number, but it is not on the sheet of numbers you have. While you could cut out individual numbers and line then up, it is very difficult to get the whole number straight. It is easier if you can find two existing numbers that, between them, have the digits you need in two blocks. For example, you need 45365 but it is not on the sheet, but it does have 45341 and 46512. You cut out the 453 from the first and the 65 from the second to make up the number. Lining up two larger decals is a lot easier than five small ones.

Cut out the decals you need from the sheet. Because most decals are on a light blue backing paper, it can be very difficult to see white ones. An enlarged printout of what is on the sheet is a big help: sometimes this is supplied, or it may be available on the manufacturer's web site. Using magnification helps.

I cut out all the decals for one side of a model and put them on, then wait thirty minutes before doing the other side. This minimizes the risk of moving one of the decals already applied when working on the other side.

Have a photograph of what you are modelling in front of you so you can see the exact position of each decal. If doing more than one wagon, try to find different photos, as there were usually

Cut round the decals you need using a scalpel, leaving the rest of the sheet intact. This way the unused decals remain in one piece in their original places, so are easy to find next time you use the sheet.

Holding each decal in a pair of tweezers, dip in water for a second or so, then place face up on a plastic lid to soak. It will take 15–60 seconds until the decal is loose on the backing paper. Do not leave the whole decal in water: if it floats off, most of the glue will get washed off, and this will almost certainly happen if you get interrupted. If you leave a soaked decal on a box lid for an hour all that happens is that it dries out and can be soaked again.

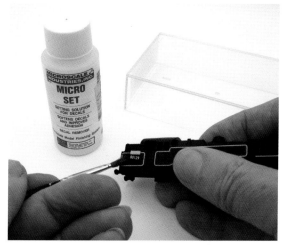

Pick up each decal with its backing paper using tweezers, and place it next to where it is to go, in the correct orientation. With the tip of a cocktail stick or a dampened paintbrush, slide the decal off the backing paper into position: provided it has soaked properly it will slide easily. Remove the backing paper with tweezers, then use the cocktail stick to push the decal into the exact position. If it will not slide, use a damp paintbrush to move it.

variations in the positions of markings between wagons.

If the decal is going on an uneven surface, for example over plank lines or panelling, when the decal is correctly positioned, roll the tip of a damp cotton bud over it, pressing down. Roll it so it does not disturb the position of the decal. As the glue dries the decal will be sucked down further. If this does not work it may be necessary to use a decal softening liquid, Micro Set for example. Dampen the area where the decal is to go with Micro Set before you put the decal on. Micro Set can be used on a decal that has not stuck properly: apply it over the dried-on decal, leave a short time for it to penetrate, then press down as before. For really difficult cases there is a much stronger softening liquid available, Micro Sol.

For decals with UV-cured ink, such as those from Railtec, the softening liquids do not work, and may make things worse. Instead, add a few drops of PVA glue to the water used to wet them when applying them to an irregular surface.

For lining, do not apply long lengths as they usually end up in a knot. Cut the lining into sections 1in (2–3cm) long, and position them so they butt up against each other. This is surprisingly easy to do. When fitting lining to an exact length it is easier to have two pieces slightly longer in total than needed, and overlap them to get the precise length.

Finally, varnish the whole model to seal the decals, and more importantly to give the model a uniform finish. I use spraycans of varnish. For freight wagons I want a very matt finish, and the best I know is Testors Dullcote, which is very matt. For passenger stock I use a matt or satin acrylic varnish, often artist's varnish. It may take more than one coat before the decals blend in.

PRINTING YOUR OWN DECALS

You will need to create artwork for the decals. For simple ones, a word processor will suffice. Note you can enter point sizes for text that are not in the drop-down boxes, for example something like 2.4pt. For more complex decals, use a package such as CorelDRAW.

Milk tank with home-printed decals. The lower part has an orange background, and the decal goes the full width of the tank. The ends are painted to match. The upper part has decals just for the logo. They were printed on clear decal paper and applied to a white-painted tank.

Additional fonts will need to be installed. There are thousands of free ones on the Internet. Search for 'Old Road Signs' (most grouping lettering), 'Gill Sans' (early BR), and 'Rail Alphabet' (BR Corporate Image). Sometimes an image can be taken from a photograph and printed out.

Some companies, for example Precision Decals and Railtec, will print decals from your artwork.

In some cases you can print your own, on decal paper in a computer printer. Decal paper comes in four types: laser or inkjet, transparent, or white background. It has a severe limitation: apart from black, the colours are transparent and only show if they are on a white or a near-white background. If you print yellow letters on transparent paper and apply it to a maroon coach, all you will see is a faint smudge. This limits you to three options:

• If only black lettering is wanted you can print on transparent decal paper.

• If the wagon is white, or very close to white, colours can be printed on transparent paper.

• Otherwise print on white decal paper with the background set to the livery colour – for example bauxite with white lettering. Either print the width of the complete side, or cut out close to the lettering so only a small amount of the background colour shows; then any slight colour difference will not be noticed.

GLAZING

For coaches, often all that is needed by way of glazing is a strip of clear plastic behind the windows. It looks good for thin etched-metal coach sides. For a model with thicker sides – as most vehicles – you need the glazing inside the frames, as a sill at a scale 6in deep looks wrong.

An easy way is to use a liquid glaze, for example Krystal Klear or Glue 'N' Glaze. This is a thick

PVA glue that dries clear. Put some on the end of a cocktail stick, run it round the inside of the frame, then drag it across with the stick held parallel to the opening so you get a film across the whole 'window'. Watch an online video if you have difficulty with this. When it dries it goes clear. Unfortunately it is not flat: it will be much thicker at the edges and will distort the light. It is better than not having glazing, but it will not look good close up.

It can be made flatter by putting masking tape over the outside of the window and applying the glazing to the inside. When the tape is removed the 'window' will be much more even, but the side against the tape will be opaque. A further layer of glaze must be added on the outside to make it clear. The end result is better, but still far from perfect.

The best way is to cut out individual rectangles of clear plastic sheet to fit each window exactly. Cut an oversize piece and gradually file it down with an emery board, until it is a tight fit. Apply small amounts of a clear-drying glue round the edges with a pin, and place in position. Most clear-drying PVA glues are suitable for this, including liquid glazes. It is tedious work, but it produces good results.

If the screen is curved, cut the glazing from a suitably curved piece of plastic – for example, the clear plastic packaging in which many consumer products are contained.

For frosted glass, glue thin tissue paper such as cigarette paper on the back. Alternatively rub the back of the glazing with a fibreglass brush in different directions to produce a light frosted effect.

If glazing gets scratched or fogged, it can usually be restored by painting over it with Pledge floor polish.

ADDING HANDRAILS

Many kits need you to add handrails. You might want to add rails to RTR stock, particularly older models, either because they are missing or to replace moulded plastic rails. In many cases it is better to add them after painting: you may want to leave them as bare metal, and they can get in the way of adding decals.

I use 0.30mm brass for brass, and 0.30mm nickel-silver wire for steel. For black-painted rails, chemically blacken a length of wire first, then cut it into sections for individual rails. For something finer or stronger, use steel guitar wire. Ernie Ball custom guitar wire comes in thicknesses from 0.008in (0.20mm) upwards. It is also useful for representing point rodding.

For short handrails, such as those by a door on a carriage or brake van, drill holes at each end of where the rail goes. Bend the wire into a U shape with sharp corners, so it fits in the holes. I hold the wire in my long-nosed pliers crossways, and bend the ends down tight to the jaws. You can vary the

The hole in the knob for the wire is usually partly blocked. To clear it, hold the knob by the stalk in pliers or a hand vice – parallel-closing pliers make a good hand vice. Locate the hole by holding it to the light, and clear it out with a small tapered reamer or a 0.3mm drill. Thread the knob on to the handrail wire – put a blob of BluTack on the other end of the wire to stop it falling off. Repeat until you have enough knobs on the wire.

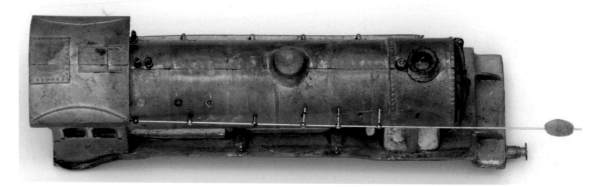

Drill 0.5mm holes for the knobs in the model. Secure the first knob on to the end of the wire with superglue, leaving the required amount of handrail sticking out beyond it. Put this into the hole nearest the cab, but do not glue. Work along, putting each knob in its hole. When complete, they can be fixed with superglue. If the resulting handrail is not quite straight, you can adjust it by gripping the head of each knob in pliers and bending it up or down.

length of the handrail according to how far down the pliers you hold the wire. You may have to reject the first few attempts.

For longer rails, such as those along a loco boiler, separate 'knobs' must be used to hold a straight length of wire. It is possible to buy brass knobs with a 0.3mm hole for the wire, that fit into a 0.5mm hole in the model, for example from N Brass.

Smaller (closer to scale) knobs can be made out of wire, filed to be half round, then wrapped round the handrail wire.

WEATHERING

Railway rolling stock is very rarely shiny clean. Even coaches have some dirt on the sides, and a lot on the underframe. Goods wagons and non-passenger stock have more: there are colour pictures of SR parcels vans where you cannot say for sure whether it is green or red! Some weathering is essential if you want a realistic appearance. If you don't want it to look really dirty, even light weathering will make it much more realistic. And it is not just rolling stock: most vehicles have some dirt, and buildings weather – there is moss on roof and walls, water stains, dirt and smoke.

Weathering is a complex area. There are complete books on it, the best known being *The Art of*

Weathering by Martyn Welch. Here, I will just run through the basics of how I go about it:

- If painting the whole model, soften the base colours by adding cream or using a very dark grey rather than black.
- Spray a general mist of 'dirt' over the model, using an airbrush, with more on the lower parts. For coaches, put a very fine mist over the upper parts, and after, wipe it off the windows with a cotton bud (but not for non-passenger stock such as parcels vans, whose windows were rarely cleaned). An airbrush is best, but if you don't have one you can paint thinned dirt colour on really dirty areas such as the chassis, and use weathering powders elsewhere.
- Apply more dirt and rust with a brush for heavy rust, stippling it on with a stiff brush. Parts can be repainted to represent a repair – for example, a single plank that has been replaced by an unpainted one. Steel wagons had panel patches welded on. These were often unpainted so rusted quickly. Most rust is a dark brown with a hint of orange. Only very recent rust is orange.
- 'Drybrush' to apply highlights, usually in a lighter colour such as a more orangey rust. To drybrush, put a little of the colour on a paintbrush, then wipe nearly all of it off on a paper towel;

On the left are the paints I mix for weathering, all Humbrol enamels: matt black (33), gunmetal (53), tarmac (122), leather (62), brown satin (133), and occasionally orange (18) and Metalcote gunmetal (27004). On the right are just a few of the many different weathering powders I use; I also have a range of greys from near white to black.

then brush over the model with light strokes. This leaves traces on any parts that stick up. It can be used for streaks down sides. I always use enamel paints for this. Rust highlights can be stippled on using a stiff brush end on, with very little paint on the brush.

• Add further patches of dirt using weathering powders. Do not put the powder directly on to the model: put some on a paper towel, then pick it up on a stiff paintbrush. Have a wide variety of colours: dirt and rust, dark greys for smoke, white for lime marks where water has dried, green/brown colours for weathering buildings.

Work with photographs in front of you, and try to produce similar effects. If working on several wagons, find different pictures as every wagon weathers differently.

Do not expect to get it perfect first time. If it looks wrong, wash it off before the paint dries, and start again. Once it looks reasonable, leave it until the next day. Then add more weathering if you think it needs it.

Some of the real experts are military modellers: look on the internet for articles and videos of more advanced techniques.

Weathered 21T hopper wagons built from NGS kits.

CHAPTER ELEVEN

EXHIBITION LAYOUTS

What makes a successful exhibition layout? Obviously it needs to be built to a high standard, but it must also appeal to visitors.

You need to keep viewers' attention. Prototypically there ought to be long periods when nothing happens, but that is not what people want to see. Nevertheless you don't have to rush things: running trains slowly adds to the sense of space. Time your trains and work out the scale speed – you are probably running them faster than you think. Coal trains rarely exceeded 20mph, which is about as slow as you can get many N-gauge locos to run. When shunting or running coaches round there would be significant pauses for uncoupling and coupling, or for the driver to check the points had changed, and that everything was safe before reversing.

It is not just trains moving that keeps people's attention: it can be loading or unloading a wagon using a crane, or a road with moving vehicles. Even if nothing moves, many viewers like to read information about what you have modelled, or even better

to hear the operator explain what is going on, and the history behind it. Modelling something people have not seen before grabs attention: it might be an industrial complex, or spectacular scenery such as a bridge.

OPERATOR POSITION

A home layout is usually operated from in front: it is mainly for you, so you might as well have the best view. However, at an exhibition this position would block the public's view, so many layouts are operated from behind. This gives good access to the fiddle yard, as well as reasonable access to the scenic area; however, you need to keep the backscene low so you can see the trains, and the sight of operators over the backscene can detract from the impact of the layout.

The layout can be operated from one or both ends, towards the front. Like this it is easy for the operator to chat to members of the public – though that can distract you from keeping things moving

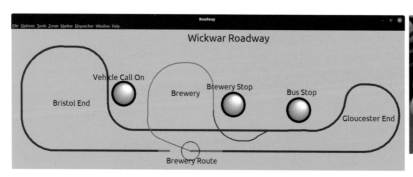

An old router box provides WiFi connectivity to the tablet that controls the roadway on Wickwar. Make the network private: if it is public then at exhibitions every phone in the building will try to connect, and this can overload the router. The box on top of the router contains a Raspberry Pi computer, using JMRI software and its built-in web server to provide the control screens. There is a main screen for controlling the vehicles, shown above, and subsidiary screens for sound effects. The Raspberry Pi interfaces to the layout via the CBUS system we use. All the software is free and readily available.

LAYOUT HEIGHT

The best viewing height for a layout is just below eye level, but your viewers vary in height from small children to tall adults. Low down, 2ft 6in to 3ft (0.8m), is a good choice if the layout is intended mainly for children, but many adults will see only the top. Slightly higher, around 3ft 6in (1m), is more common: it is low enough for people in wheelchairs and most children to see, with small children needing to use hop-ups. Higher still, 4ft to 4ft 6in (1.2–1.4m), will mean that most adults get a good view, but wheelchair users might need to use a periscope; you should provide periscopes at exhibitions if you choose this option. While tall people can bend down, some find it difficult. A further consideration is to use a height that is convenient for you when operating and working on the layout at home.

on the layout. But as an exhibition manager I have a preference for this style of operation, as it engages the public more.

If you have wireless controls the operator can move around, and mingle with viewers. We do this for the road system on Wickwar, using a tablet connected by WiFi; it is very successful, as you can explain things to the public while you operate.

Alternatively a mix of operator positions can be used.

VIDEO DISPLAYS

We use pin-hole cameras on Wickwar to provide alternative views of the layout to the public. The cameras are small and can be hidden in any building with just a 3mm hole for the lens. The views look real because they are from where you might be standing, not from several hundred yards away and high up. The best view on Wickwar is from the foot of the embankment looking up. We have four

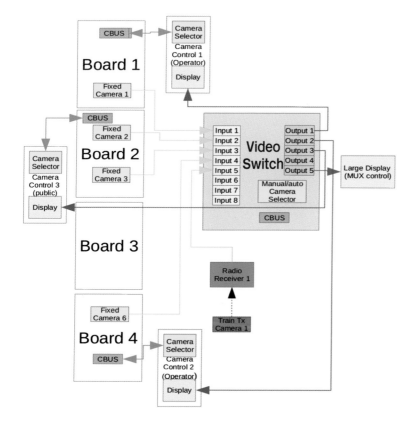

A diagram of the video system on Wickwar. The switchbox is built round an eight input/ six output video-switch matrix chip costing a few pounds. It is connected to the boards via SCART cables and controlled by the CBUS system we use on the layout. The six cameras use the PAL standard, and the field of view varies from 60 to 170 degrees.

cameras in the scenic area, and viewers can select between them.

We have two more cameras, one above each end of the fiddle yard. The picture is displayed on a small screen next to the operator at the other end, allowing them to follow trains that are out of sight at the far end of the layout.

Miniature video cameras are cheap, and small monitors are affordable. The installation on Wickwar comprises two large and two small monitors, six cameras, and two boxes with buttons to switch the view showing. The whole set-up cost under £200, most of which was for the two large monitors.

OPERATING TO A SEQUENCE

Many layouts can be operated without any particular sequence or timetable, but it makes it easier for operators if the trains are run in a fixed order. It means that when operators are swopped, they can take over quickly: they just need to know where they are in the sequence.

An end-to-end layout or terminus, or a layout with a lot of shunting, often requires a fixed sequence of moves to ensure stock is in the right position for the next move.

Wickwar is a simple 'roundy-roundy' with about twelve trains in each direction. We run trains in a set order, except when we switch the layout lighting to night time, when we switch to running the trains that have lights. Each operator has a list of the trains, which says what type of service each represents. This can be seen by viewers as well.

Displaying the sequence to the public adds interest: they know what is coming next, and can look out for it. A simple way is to have the inside of a ring binder mounted above the layout and facing upwards, with A4 sheets of card that hang down on each side. A card at the back can be flipped over so it goes to the front. The front of each sheet has a description of the next train or trains for the public to read, while the back (what would be the facing page) has a more detailed set of instructions for the operator.

More complicated, but more impressive, is to emulate the displays on the real railway. You

The 4mm-scale layout 'Shelvington and Rydes Hill' has a fully working model of a flap-type display to show what the next train is. These displays were once common at major stations.

could, for example, use an old tablet to display information in a similar format to train displays at stations. If you enjoy programming and electronics, you can buy LED alphanumeric displays in various sizes.

RELIABLE OPERATION

An exhibition layout has to run significantly better than a home layout. The trains need to run without derailing, stalling or uncoupling, and it is important to avoid operator errors and crashes.

Keep electrical systems as separate as possible, so if there is a short on one track it does not affect all the rest. You can have separate power districts for DCC, or should be able to isolate an area on DC. Allow simple operation to continue even if there is a serious fault – for example, allow trains to run in a circle even if you cannot change any points.

Before each exhibition we clean all the track and follow up with a hand-held vacuum cleaner to remove any debris. After each exhibition I clean the wheels of every loco ready for the next, and about once a year I clean the wheels of all my stock.

If a loco is running poorly or a wagon seems to be dragging, it is probably an accumulation of old oil and dust. The best solution is to strip it down, clean it thoroughly, and reassemble it with light lubrication.

I use cotton buds for cleaning locos and other stock. Use the type with small heads and a hard, firm bud; the more common ones with a large fluffy bud should be avoided, as they are difficult to get into tight corners and tend to leave as much fluff as they remove. I buy my buds from Muji, who has shops in many major UK cities and sells online. Even smaller buds are available from Tamiya, and are available at model shops and online.

All new layouts and stock will have problems: you have to keep working on eliminating them. Whenever something goes wrong, try to work out why, and fix it. At exhibitions keep a list of all the problems that occur and work through them afterwards.

Keep the trains the same from one exhibition to the next. Keep the same loco on each train, so you know it can pull it. Keep the order of the wagons or coaches the same, as swapping them round can lead to uncoupling.

An easy way to achieve this is to have all your exhibition trains in stock boxes, stored by train with each labelled. If you introduce a new train, run it for ten minutes on the layout before the exhibition to make sure it is reliable.

Take a few spare locos to the exhibition in case one fails, and a few spare wagons and coaches.

Cramer bath rubbers make excellent track cleaners. They leave fewer bits than many of the track rubbers sold for model railways. Each can be cut into two or three pieces. They are available from stores that sell plumbing hardware.

I use Slater's track cleaner or isopropyl alcohol (IPA) for most cleaning. In principle they might affect some paint finishes, but I have never had a problem. I sometimes use lighter fuel instead, as it evaporates quickly. If something more powerful is needed I use cellulose thinners, but these can damage paintwork if they come in contact.

Once stock has been cleaned, it will benefit from lubrication. For locos I use an 'electrically conductive' oil such as MaGeR from N Brass. These oils are not conductive in bulk, but only in thin layers, such as between a pick-up and a wheel. They act as a contact enhancer, giving better electrical connection. For plastic components that need lubrication I use a Teflon lubricant from Faller – oil can go gummy and make things even worse. Graphite powder can be used instead for lubricating plastic; I use it on couplings when they are sticky. For an electrical switch that is not working well, spray it with a switch cleaner that includes a contact enhancer. It is useful for keyboards and noisy switches on Hi-Fi as well as the layout.

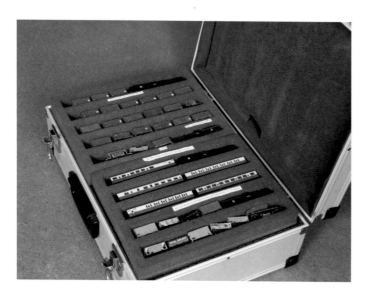

Instrument cases (flight cases) make excellent stock boxes, light and robust. I use foam trays sold by J B Modelworld to hold the stock. Each tray holds ten or twelve coaches. My case is 44 × 33 × 16cm (17 × 13 × 6in) and holds eight trays, or for Wickwar, about twelve trains and a few spare vehicles. Always put locos at the hinge side so they are at the bottom when you lift the case and do not crush other stock. Each tray is labelled with the train that goes in it, and the fiddle-yard road and position where it goes when the layout is up. This makes set-up at an exhibition much faster. The trains are put in the box in order, right to left, top to bottom.

ACCIDENTAL UNCOUPLING AND DERAILMENTS

If a wagon uncouples or a loco derails it is not necessarily the fault of the stock: often it is as much a problem with the track. Watch next time to see just what happened and where. A wheel can derail and the train run without apparent problems for some time, until it gets to the next set of points.

If stock uncouples, first check that the couplings are not twisted or drooping, and that close-coupling mechanisms move freely. If a coupling is obviously faulty and not easy to fix, remove the wagon from the train for attention after the exhibition. Otherwise, try turning one or both of the wagons that uncouple around, or change the order within the train. Sometimes a small bead of BluTack to hold the coupling arm horizontal will sort out the problem temporarily. Have a few spare couplings with you; NEM ones can be swapped over.

If you are having problems with stock that ran well at the previous exhibition, probably one of the board joints is not correctly aligned. Check the track at each joint, both visually for side-to-side displacement, and with a finger for vertical alignment. A small vertical displacement often causes leading bogies to derail.

If a particular point or connector has an issue regularly, then make the decision to re-lay or rewire it.

REDUCING OPERATOR ERRORS: CONTROLS AND AUTOMATION

Even the smallest layout needs at least one relief operator at exhibitions. For a home layout, it doesn't matter much if a switch is in the wrong place on the control panel or works the opposite way to the others – it is your layout and you know its quirks. Nor do you have to label them all. But unless the controls are well laid out and consistent, other

Rapido couplings, if not absolutely horizontal, are liable to uncouple at any slight unevenness in the track. Much smaller deviations than shown will cause uncoupling. I would expect the two shown to uncouple frequently at an exhibition, even paired with level couplings. The problem most often occurs on kits using a Peco chassis, like these two. When building, check that the couplings sit level before gluing the chassis to the body, and adjust if needed: for example, add paper to the bottom of the plug on the body that pushes the coupling down if the coupling is drooping, or file the plug down if the coupling is sticking up. The problem with the wagon on the left can be seen clearly: the body is not tight against the chassis, so the plug on the body that holds the coupling down is out of position. If glued properly the coupling would be level. It is possible to lower a coupling that is high by slicing a little off the lip of the pocket, or if drooping, put a raised nick in the lower lip with a knife. For some 'repeat offenders' I simply glue the coupling solid.

people will find it very frustrating to operate, and may not volunteer a second time.

While it is possible to operate points and signals from a DCC handset, it requires the operator to be familiar with dozens of codes. It is far better to have a mimic panel showing the track layout, with buttons or switches in appropriate places for points and signals. Control panels should be as simple and straightforward as possible: any additional switches will get operated by accident sooner or later. Rarely used controls, such as those for points in the goods yard that are only used when shunting, might be better moved to a separate panel.

Any essential information, such as DCC loco numbers, or which trains should go on a particular route, should be written down and displayed next to the panel.

At an exhibition operators will get distracted by questions and are more likely to make mistakes, and train crashes while someone is watching are embarrassing, so any locking and automation that can be provided to reduce operator errors helps. Here are some examples:

- Route setting, where a single button sets a whole series of points correctly. Most DCC systems and layout buses allow you to program this. With stud and probe systems a diode matrix can be used.
- Isolate the track before a junction when the points are set against, to avoid crashes.
- Indicator lights to show whether the fiddle yard is clear, or which way a point is set.
- A flashing indicator light when a point is set in an unusual position, which might cause crashes if not reset before the next train.
- Train-on-track detectors to prevent a train being sent into a road that is already occupied, or to prevent points being changed when a train is passing over them, or to remind the operator of a train that is out of sight.
- Automation of signals, so they change automatically in a plausible manner.

On many layouts the most complex area to operate is the fiddle yard, and it is also the most repetitive so mistakes are likely. Crashes in the fiddle yard can

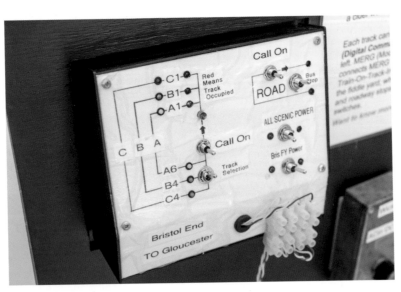

The control panels on Wickwar are very simple, with only two switches normally used: a three-way switch to select the fiddle-yard road, and a call on switch. Lights indicate track occupancy in the fiddle yard. Two emergency switches turn off power if there is a problem, such as a derailment blocking another line. Two more switches control the roadway, but are only used if the WiFi-connected tablet is not working.

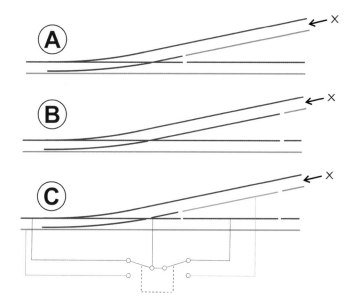

Diagram A shows the normal way of wiring a point with an electrified crossing, with isolation gaps just past the crossing. If the point is set as shown, a train approaching from X will derail on the point and possibly even hit another train. By moving the isolation gap further away, as shown in B, this can be prevented. The train now has time to stop after it crosses the gap before it reaches the point. However, when it crosses the gap it will short across, and on DCC, stop everything in the same power district. If you are using a switch to power the crossing, then a two-pole switch can isolate the rail leading up to the point, as shown in C (green wire). If the point is set against, the train will stop without shorting the power.

derail several trains. Time and effort spent on automating the fiddle yard will repay itself, and operation will be more reliable and enjoyable.

SAFETY CONSIDERATIONS

Keep all mains power away from the layout. Mount all the power supplies needed for the layout in an

The Wickwar power boxes. The lower one supplies power to the layout, and the top one power for the LED lighting. Note the green stickers, indicating they have been PAT safety tested: exhibitions require this, and many will do it for you.

earthed metal box, or use CE-certified plug-type power supplies. Rather than using 240V lights, use LED lights powered from a 12V supply.

Make a black cloth 'skirt' to go round the bottom of the boards, attached with Velcro, to hide the supports. It must be made fire-resistant by spraying it with 'fire-retardant spray', sold by all the large DIY stores and online.

LIGHTING

At home you may have fixed lighting for your layout area, though it is best to have lights for the layout, rather than rely on the room lights.

For an exhibition layout, unless you provide lighting you are at the mercy of the exhibition hall, with anything from direct sunlight in an atrium to dim lights in a windowless drama studio. The colour of the light can vary as well: a layout that looks good under warm indoor lights can look washed out under sunlight, and colours can appear far more intense than usual under some artificial lights.

So plan to include lighting as part of your layout. The best lighting is bright light (similar to sunlight) at least 1 foot (30cm) in front of the layout, supplemented by warmer and less strong lighting over the centre of the layout to reduce shadows.

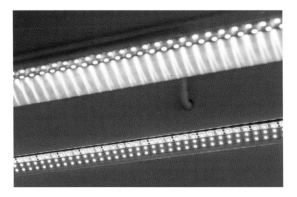

Wickwar has three rows of LED striplights in front, two bright white and one warm white, and two further strips of warm white over the centre.

We can run Wickwar in 'moonlit' mode, with just a single strip of bright white lights for illumination, to show off our lit trains, buildings and vehicles.

LED light strips are a good way to provide illumination. A 12V power supply of several hundred watts is needed to drive them. Avoid fluorescent lights as they need mains voltage on the layout and are more likely to fail. Spotlights are not recommended as they form pools of light that look unnatural.

A gantry is needed on which to mount the lights. It can be made from aluminium tube and angle, light and strong.

Wickwar has a cloth canopy above the lights, primarily to block ambient light when we are running in night-time mode. In halls with direct sunlight the canopy reduces outside light on the layout, which otherwise can make colours look washed out.

PRESENTATION

Viewers become more involved and enjoy your layout more if it is well presented. When you are next at an exhibition, look at layouts similar to the one you are building to get ideas.

Many layouts use a 'proscenium arch' style, where the viewable part of the layout is surrounded by a blank panel on each side and a beam across the top, so the whole creates a frame around the layout. It concentrates viewers' attention on the layout, and cuts out the distractions of what is happening behind the scenes.

Display the name of the layout prominently. It can be a painted board across the top of layout. I prefer a vinyl roll-up banner a few inches deep, as it is easier to transport. Use Velcro to attach it to your lighting rig.

There will be blank spaces, for example on the sides of the layout or below the front, where you can display information about the layout and what it

Wickwar's gantry comprises a vertical rectangular tube each side of the layout, level with the front, with T pieces on top that support aluminium angle strip with LED lights glued on. The strips come apart in the centre so they are short enough to fit in an estate car.

Garden waste bag
used to transport
backscene

Video Screen
Selection push
buttons on right

Information
Trains, Maps
History

WICKWAR

Pull-Up Displays
Left club info
Right Wickwar photos

Fireproof Curtain
Modern pictures of
buildings modelled

Demo Table
Faller test track
Reprints of articles

Wickwar at Alexandra Palace during set-up. This venue insists that their own heavy-duty barriers are used. Smaller venues allow you to use your own barriers, and might not even provide any of their own. For preference we use our own lightweight barriers in front of the layout.

If you have modelled a real location, put pictures in appropriate positions along the front. It makes the point that it is a real location, and people like to compare your model and the original. This is 'Langston Bridge' by Julian Thornhill.

portrays. Say where the tracks going off-scene lead to. Provide a large-scale map of the area showing the surrounding towns. For transport, display boards can be clipped inside the box lids.

When we took Wickwar to exhibitions the questions asked showed us what people wanted to know. The displays now are completely different to what we started with. Many people want to know just where in the country the layout is set. To provide extra display space we made a pull-up vinyl banner. Provided you put the images together yourself they are not expensive. A second banner has information about our club and goes out with all our club layouts.

A table can be used alongside the layout to display more information or to give demonstrations. We have a demo of the Faller car system, historical pictures, and reprints of articles about the layout, such as how the backscene was made.

GOING TO EXHIBITIONS

First of all you have to obtain an invitation from the exhibition manager. Unless you are a well known modeller with a track record, it is difficult to get invitations to the big shows without the manager seeing the layout. Local shows are easier and will lead to invites to other shows. In any case, it is better to go to a small local show first, as there are sure to be problems to sort out.

To advertise what you are offering, you should produce an 'Information for Exhibition Managers' document. A good format is a double-sided A4 sheet. On the front, have a couple of pictures and a

WICKWAR – Farnham and District Model Railway Club (F&DMRC

Information for Exhibition Managers

We prefer an area not in direct sunlight for our dusk/night running, we have full lighting so a dark area is fine.

In addition to the layout we want to have an information/demo table one side or the other, preferably viewable from the side, to display historic and current photos of the site, a small demo of the Faller car, samples of the Styrofoam baseboards, Scupltamold scenery and backscene material, and a demo of the electronics used.

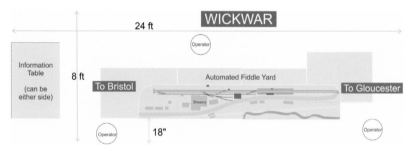

Layout name	Wickwar
Owner	Farnham and District MRC
Scale/Gauge	British N, 1:148
Area/Era	BR(M) early 50s
Contact	ngauge@farnhammrc.org.uk
Layout size	17' x 3' 6"
Space required	24' x 8'. Operated from both sides at front, with fiddle yard attendant at rear, and information/demo table on one side or the other of the layout.
Viewable area	Central scenic section is 12 feet wide.
Layout type	Twin track oval.
Operators	6
Expenses	Can be transported in 2 estate cars, expenses being just fuel, with one more car for operators and possibly some rail fares.
	Accommodation is likely to be required if more than 50 miles from Aldershot, 2 twins and 2 singles. For these shows we usually hire a small van (£110) and take 1 additional car.
Power	5A (13A socket) required.
Barriers	We will bring our own unless you want us to use yours
Lighting	Included.
Tables/Chairs	4 chairs, no tables needed.
Insurance value	14,000 (layout £4,000; stock £10,000).
Availability	1 or 2 day shows
More	Details and photographs: www.farnhammrc.co.uk/?page_id=3

The reverse side of the Wickwar information sheet, with the information for exhibition managers.

description of the layout that is suitable for inclusion in a show guide; on the reverse, give all the details that the exhibition manager needs: the size of the layout and the operating area, with a plan showing the viewable parts, how many operators there are, and the likely transport costs.

Take copies to local exhibitions, or email them to exhibition managers. Larger exhibitions book most exhibits at least a year in advance, so start touting for invites before the layout is complete (but far enough along that you are confident it will be fit to exhibit!). If you have access to a web site, put details and photos there, and the fact sheet for download. When you do go to an exhibition take plenty of copies of the information sheet to give to anyone interested. Keep a diary of invitations and dates.

It is all too easy to forget something when going to an exhibition, so be well organized. Store all the smaller items you need in a number of 'Really Useful' boxes: cables, removable items of scenery, control panels, a few tools for repairs. Put a label on top of each box, saying what should be in it. Have a packing list of all the boxes and layout components you need to take.

One of the many boxes that goes with Wickwar to exhibitions.

INDEX